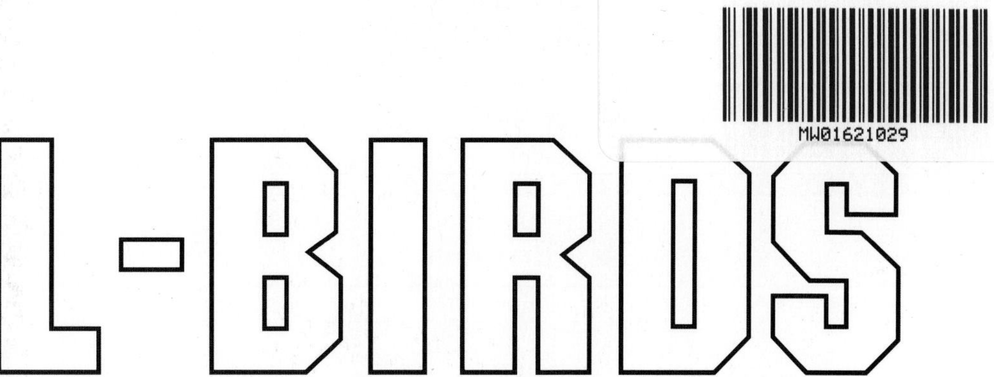

American Combat Liaison Aircraft of World War II

Terry M. Love

FLYING BOOKS INTERNATIONAL
121 5th Avenue NW • New Brighton, MN 55112
1-800-225-5575

L-BIRDS

American Combat Liaison Aircraft of World War II

By Terry M. Love

FLYING BOOKS INTERNATIONAL, Publishers & Wholesalers
121 5th Avenue NW, Suite 300
New Brighton, MN 55112
800-225-5575
G.E. Herrick, Publisher

Mystery Ship
by Edward H. Phillips

Wings of Stearman
by Peter M. Bowers

The Staggerwing Story
by Edward H. Phillips

Mr. Piper And His Cubs
by Devon Francis

Piper: A Legend Aloft
by Edward H. Phillips

Beechcraft, Pursuit of Perfection
by Edward H. Phillips

Cessna, A Master's Expression
by Edward H. Phillips

Travel Air, Wings Over the Prairie
by Edward H. Phillips

Wings of Cessna, Model 120 to the Citation X
by Edward H. Phillips

Speed, the Biography of Charles Holman
by Noel E. Allard

The 91 Before Lindbergh
by Peter Allen

DH-88: The Story of DeHavilland's Racing Comets
by David Ogilvy

The New Ryan
by Ev Cassagneres

T-Hangar Tales
by Joseph P. Juptner

L-BIRDS
American Combat Liaison Aircraft of World War II

FLYING BOOKS INTERNATIONAL,
Publishers & Wholesalers
121 5th Avenue NW, Suite 300
New Brighton, MN 55112

Library of Congress Cataloging in Publication Data

Love, Terry M.

L-birds: American combat liaison aircraft of World War II / by Terry M. Love.

p. cm

Includes index.

ISBN 0-911139-31-151995

1. Combat liaison airplanes--United States--History. 2. World War, 1939-1945--Aerial operations, American. 3. United States. Army--Aviation--History--20th century. I. Title.
UG1242.A27 L68 2001
623.7'46--dc21

2001023266

Front cover illustration: *A Stinson L-5, 42-98451, of the 25th Liaison Squadron, 13th Air Force, scouts over the Philippine countryside in the early Spring of 1945. The "Guinea Short Lines" all had white tails and green/yellow/green stripes applied to the wings and tail, for unit markings and easier recognition.*

Cover and side-view illustrations: *John Valo*

Rear cover illustration: *A Marine OY-1 of VMO-3 over Hagushi Harbor anchorage, just off the island of Okinawa in 1945 shows the backseat observer pointing downward at the large fleet gathered there. The number 51 above a white circle on the tail plus unidentifiable nose art, are the only markings on the Stinson. (David Manley collection)*

Printed and bound in the United States of America
Art Director, Noel Allard
Publisher, G.E. Herrick

TABLE OF CONTENTS

ACKNOWLEDGMENTS

I especially want to thank my very patient wife, Carol Love, for putting up with me doing all of my letters, post office runs, photo lab errands, multiple phone calls, etc. She is the best!

I would also like to thank the following other sources of information found during the research for this book, even though I may not have utilized the data. One source was the book, "The Stinsons," by John W. Underwood, published by Heritage Press of Glendale, California, and the other source was Bill Stratton of ILPA.

DEDICATION

To all former liaison pilots of World War II. You guys maybe did not make all of the headlines, but you made the difference between life and death to thousands of very grateful GIs on the ground.

CREDITS

Noel Allard
Bill Horn
National World War II Glider Pilots Association
Tom Hind
James V. Crow
James H. Brodie
Jacque Drabier
U.S. Army Aviation Museum

INTRODUCTION

Take The High Ground

For centuries past to the present, a prudent military commander has always tried to "take the high ground"—this, of course, is learned in Military Science 101! History has many examples of the importance of height so a commander can overlook the enemy and his movements. Castles and forts were built in cleared areas atop hills so all who approached could be seen and scrutinized. To defend against Indian raids, early American settlers built forts with high wooden palisades and look-out towers. In the battle for the Alamo, General Santa Ana of the Mexican Army directed his forces from the bell tower of nearby San Fernando Cathedral. At Monterrey, General Zachary Taylor commanded from the ridge of mountains circling that city. During the Civil War, General Robert E. Lee ordered General Pickett's charge up Cemetery Ridge at the Battle of Gettysburg. And Teddy Roosevelt's charge up San Juan Hill during the Spanish-American War, has a special place in history.

From lofty heights, a military commander can also keep track of his own troops for maneuvering. With the invention of the howitzer, there was an added requirement for observing hits in order to zero-in the artillery. Then in the late 1700s, the invention of the balloon by Montgolfier brothers in France, offered the military leader a way of putting up a high observation post at the exact point where he needed it. Almost immediately, the military powers of Europe recognized the usefulness of the balloon and, in 1784, the French began using captive hydrogen balloons for observation.

The United States Army followed suit, making successful use of observation balloons in both the Civil War, and in the Spanish-American Wars. In 1907, the Army sent out a specification for a military airplane which resulted in their obtaining a Wright Flyer. With the Wright Brothers, Langley and others, a new era in aerial activity arrived. Few realized or even imagined the aeroplane could have so profound an effect of peoples' lives. True enough, for many years men had dreamed of imitating birds, but in the early 1900s that wish became reality. Suddenly, man no longer had been content with merely gliding or soaring, he could actually take off, fly and land at will.

The U.S. military took delivery of a few Wright Flyers in 1909. The very first U.S. Army aircraft was assigned to the Signal Corps solely to climb to altitude, look around, return and report on enemy activity—the first observation plane. Lieutenant Benjamin Foulois was Orville Wright's first passenger on the Army's first aircraft. As Foulois related it, Orville offered him that unique opportunity not because of his "intellectual and technical ability" but because he was short, slender, and knew how to read a map. For the young Lieutenant, that ride marked the beginning of a lifelong affair with flying.

In 1910, he became the Army's one-man air force when the War Department ordered him to take the Wright Flyer to Ft. Sam Houston in San Antonio, Texas, and teach himself to fly. Probably the only military aviator to win his wings by means of a "correspondence course," Lieutenant Foulois would telegraph the Dayton, Ohio inventors after each of a continuing series of crack-ups, soliciting their advice of questions of piloting techniques. He survived the bumps to become the Army Air Service's first pilot instructor.

Over the next ten years, the US Army slowly built up an air section made up of both lighter-than-air and heavier-than-aircraft, all directed at the role of the observation. The first combat role of the observation aeroplane came in 1912 when the Wright Flyer scouted Pancho Villa's border raiders for General Pershing.

American aviation pioneer Glenn Curtiss began dropping dummy bombs on the outline of a battleship, and in October of 1911, the Italians first used an aeroplane for aerial reconnaissance, which had become the primary role envisaged by the armies for the new invention when World War I broke out.

At the onset of hostilities, Germany had the largest air force in the world, comprising of some 260 aircraft, most of which were observation types. France had about 160 planes, but despite inferiority in numbers, had an advanced aviation industry that would prove capable of producing steadily improving aircraft to meet the needs of its own fighting services, and to build them in sufficient quantity to supply a fair percentage of the needs of it allies, also. Britain managed to produce 63 aircraft for its Royal Flying Corps in France, their pilots flying across the English Channel during mid-August 1914.

Before World War I, most army commanders had shown little interest in aircraft. They all agreed they were a handy way to carry urgent messages and that, subject to weather, they might prove to be a good observation platform. Because that attitude prevailed, the 500-plus aircraft British, France, and Germany had manufactured before the war began, were mostly intended for observation and scouting. Early in the hostilities, it was proved that they were very valuable in that role. Not only did they provide army commanders with frequently updated information on the enemy, they could also direct artillery to new standards of accuracy and efficiency. The early planes were so valuable it became necessary to prevent enemy aircraft from access to the airspace above and to the rear of one's line of defense. From that first period awareness the aeroplane quickly developed as a well-rounded offensive as well a defensive weapon.

Local field commanders used captive hydrogen balloons in the war, for observation and artillery spotting, but newly developed, armed aircraft soon turned them into flaming death-traps. Thus the utility of the observation aeroplane!

The airplane came out of World War I a real and proven weapon. Fighter and bomber pilots were written up in newspapers, but the observation crews got scant recognition. After the war, the Air Corps had the capability of creating publicity in peacetime through air races, record-breaking flights, and flight demonstrations. On the other hand, the ground forces could do nothing but occasionally march in a parade!

This Air Corps publicity generated funding which was used to develop the airplane even further. As in combat, the bulk of publicity was generated by the fighters and bombers, not observation aircraft. Moreover, promotions and positions tended to be given to fighter and bomber crews, not observation crews. The Air Corps, being officially part of the Army, did pay token service by providing some observation squadrons, but being assigned to these was considered little more than penalty duty. Actual command of the observation squadrons was always a battle with the Chief of the Air Corps wanting to maintain control of all aircraft, while the Army ground commanders felt they should have direct command of the observation planes assigned to support them, and, until 1941, the ground commanders always won.

As a result, the Army field commanders of 1940, were little better off for observation than their predecessors had been a century before in the Mexican War.

The standard Air Corps observation plane at the end of the 1930s, was the North American O-47. A 1,000HP Wright Cyclone engine powered the O-47, which looked like a pot-bellied AT-6 Texan. The three-seat aircraft had a 6,035 pound empty weight, and a 8,312 pound gross weight. It could top off at 240 MPH, cruise at 218 MPH, and land at 67 MPH. But it flew too fast for a good frontline observation aircraft, and required the hard runways of an established airbase. Thus it was really useless.

Enter the coming war in Europe by the late thirties, the Louisiana War Games, and the Light aircraft, and we have the birth of Army Aviation!

United States Army Aviation

The following is the general order creating U. S. Army Aviation—the order by which created the thousands of L-Birds, utility aircraft and the thousands of helicopters used in the Korean War, the Vietnam War, and all of the other operations participated in by the U S Army.

WDGCT 320.2 (2-5-42) June 6, 1942

MEMORANDUM FOR THE COMMANDING GENERAL, ARMY GROUND FORCES

Subject: Organic Air Observation for Field Artillery.

1. Reference is made to letter War Department, February 25, 1942, AG 320.2 (2-5-42) MT-C, subject: Service Test of Organic Air Observation for Field Artillery, and 1st Endorsement, thereto.

2. Your recommendation that organic air observation units be included in Field Artillery organizations is approved.

3. It is desired that you take immediate steps to effect the necessary changes in organization, equipment and training entailed by the action. The following will govern:

a. Organization:
   (1) Liaison airplanes will be authorized for Field Artillery units at the rate of 2 per light and medium Artillery Battalion, 2 per Division Artillery Headquarters and Headquarters Battery or Field Artillery Brigade Headquarters and Headquarters Battery.
   (2) Personnel will be authorized at the rate of 1 pilot and 1/2 airplane mechanic for each liaison plane authorized.
   (3) The required changes in T/Os and T-BAs will be submitted as soon as practicable.

b. Procurement and Maintenance:
   (1) The Commanding General, Army Air Forces will be responsible for the procurement and issue of airplanes, spare parts, repair materials, and the necessary auxiliary flying equipment required by this program. The airplanes will be commercial low performance aircraft of the "Piper Cub" type.
   (2) All maintenance other than that requiring the facilities of base shops will be accomplished by the Army Ground Forces.
   (3) Maintenance requiring the facilities of base shops (customarily referred to as 3rd echelon maintenance in the Army Air Forces) will be a responsibility of the Commanding General, Army Air Forces.
   (4) It is desired that you confer with the Commanding General, Army Air Forces regarding the number of aircraft required under the 1942 Troop Basis, the anticipated delivery rate, the established requirements of spare parts, repair materials and auxiliary equipment, as well as the procedures and policies regarding their issue and delivery.

c. Personnel
   (1) Qualifications: Recommendations for the detailed qualifications and specifications for both commissioned and enlisted personnel will be submitted for approval. These will fall into two general categories: a pilot capable of piloting the liaison-type airplane as well as assisting in normal maintenance; and a mechanic qualified to service the airplane and perform repairs incident to 1st. and 2nd echelon maintenance.
   (2) Sources of personnel:
      (a) Pilots: Volunteers, now under your control, who are qualified to pilot liaison-type airplanes be utilized to the maximum as pilots. Additional pilots needed to fill requirements of the 1942 Troop Basis will be made available by the Commanding General, Army Air Forces.
      (b) Mechanics: Mechanics will be procured from sources under your control.
   (3) Extra compensation and ratings:
      (a) Pilots will be authorized additional compensation for participation in frequent and regular aerial flights. A rating generally similar to that of a liaison pilot will be established for pilots.
      (b) Appropriate ratings for mechanics may be Technician, Grade 3, or lower.

d. Training:
   (1) The basic flight training for pilots (exclusive

of those under your command already qualified) will be a responsibility of the Commanding General, Army Air Forces. This training will be limited to that necessary to enable safe operation of low performance aircraft and qualify a student according to standards established for liaison pilots.

(2) You are authorized to organize at Fort Sill, Oklahoma, or other stations selected by you, a course of instruction for the operational training of pilots, mechanics, and observers in the tactical employment of organic air observation in Field Artillery units.

4. Changes in training literature will be prepared at the earliest practical date.

5. A copy of the directive to the Commanding Gerneral, Army Air Forces, is attached hereto. The Commanding General, Army Air Forces, has been furnished a copy of this letter.

By order of the Secretary of War:
I. H. Edwards
Brigadier General,
Assistant Chief of Staff

CHAPTER ONE

The Birth of Army Aviation

Over sixty years ago, America was mobilizing for an all-out war effort against the Axis. At Fort Sill, Oklahoma, the Artillery School was a scene of intense activity. But, in odd contrast to the surrounding hustle and bustle, a small group of Army officers and enlisted men patiently marked time as they participated in limited flight and maintenance training programs. These men were waiting for a decision on the results of a test—a test which led to the birth of Army Aviation, and the thousands of helicopters and aircraft that would follow! They had evaluated the concept of using light aircraft organic to the Field Artillery to spot targets. After-action reports had been waiting and hoping they had convinced the War Department that the artillery needed its own light aircraft quickly and effectively detect targets hidden to ground observers.

During the Louisiana War Games in 1941, Piper Aircraft, at not cost to the U. S. Government, provided some new Piper J-3 Cubs to the military to prove that they could be valuable ARMY assets. Barely visible is the civilian registration NC on top of the right wing. The cross on the fuselage was red. The name and insignia of the "Grasshopper" first appeared here during the war games. The mounted-horse cavalry was rendered obsolete by armor and aircraft. (NASM)

The group was rewarded for its efforts and patience when the War Department approved organic aviation for the Field Artillery on June 6, 1942. This date is now officially recognized as the birthday of Army Aviation.

In the history of Army Aviation, 1907 was an important year. An Aeronautical Division in the office of the Chief Signal Officer was established on August 1, and the United States became the first country to contract for a military airplane when the Signal Corps called for bids in December of 1907. On August 20, 1908, the Wright brothers brought their Flyer, a modified version of the 1905 airplane, to Fort Myer, Virginia for testing.

It was a pusher type with the motor and prop located behind the pilot and passenger. On September 3, 1908, the first flight, lasting one minute and 11 seconds, was made. This flight, the first of an airplane on a military installation in America, was followed by a series of test flights that were highlighted on the afternoon of September 9, when Orville remained aloft for one hour, two minutes and fifteen seconds.

Just as success seemed imminent, tragedy struck at Fort Myer. On September 17, 1908, Orville invited Lt. Thomas Selfridge, an official Army observer at the trials, to ride as a passenger on a test flight. On the

During the Louisiana War Games, various types of camouflage were tried out . Usually washable paints were used. This North American 0-47 has not had its insignias painted on yet. Note the exhaust pipe is fitted with an additional length for flame dampening for night operations. This observation aircraft was practically useless for Army liaison-type mission, as discovered during the war games. (Minnesota Air Guard Museum)

As discovered during the Louisiana War Games, the Curtis 0-52 Owl was, also, practically useless for Army liaison missions. Both the 0-52 and the 0-47 required large technical support, aviation fuel, hard runways, and they were expensive. They flew too fast to observe details and items on the ground, and they were maintenance-intensive a mechanical nightmare. (NASM)

fourth turn of field, one of the prop blades struck a brace wire attached to the rudder. The airplane fell 150 feet and hit the ground. Lt. Selfridge was killed—the first man to give his life in powered flight. Selfridge Air Base, near Detroit, was named for him.

The following year, the Wright Brothers returned to Fort Myer. Lt. Benjamin Foulois flew with Orville on a test flight on July 30. The tests were successful and the Army accepted the airplane on August 2. It became U.S. Army aeroplane number one! As a part of the contract, the Wrights trained a Lt. Frederick Humphreys, among others, to fly the aircraft. Lt. Humphreys soloed first and became the first Army aviator.

Three Army lieutenants, Paul Beck, G. Kelly, and John Walker, were trained by Glenn Curtiss. They joined Lt. Foulois in Texas in April of 1911. On May 10, 1911 Lt. Kelly was killed in a crash and became the first training fatality. Kelly Field in Texas, is named after him.

By November of 1912, the Army had 12 pilots, 39 enlisted men, and 12 airplanes. It was then that the Army first used airplanes for observation and artillery adjustments. At the request of the Field Artillery Board, two aircraft were sent to Fort Riley, Kansas for experiments.

On July 18, 1914 Congress created an Aviation Section within the Signal Corps. The Aviation Section increased Army Aviation strength and scope, gave it a definite status, attracted top grade personnel, and gave manufacturers much needed experiments.

During World War I, the Army had 39 aero squadrons participating in action. Reconnaissance and artillery fire missions were a priority. When the war was over, the AEF returned home and with them came new ideas on the use of the airplane. One of the new concepts was Army Aviation.

Disagreements between the Air Corps and the ground forces grew. The Air Corps was rapidly developing its concepts of strategic air warfare, and its entire ground support program weakened. By the end of the 1930s, Artillery officers, especially, fired an increasing barrage of demands for more effective aerial fire direction. When these demands were not satisfied by the standard Air Corps observation squadrons, Artillery officers began looking at light aircraft organic to the units which they served.

In May of 1940, President Franklin Roosevelt's request for 50,000 aircraft a year, created a meeting of light plane manufacturers and the military. Army and Navy officers told the manufacturers that there would be no place for the light plane in the coming war effort. Ed Porterfield asked: "General, will there be any place in the program for light airplanes?"

"No," replied the general, "at least not in the Army or Air Corps. They're impractical for military use."

"How about the Navy?"

"I'm afraid not," answered a naval captain.

It was then that William Piper said, "It seems to me that the lightplane hasn't been given a chance to show what it can do. Now that we're here, we'd like to explain our views of the picture so somebody, some sergeant or corporal, maybe."

It had taken some politics and practical demonstrations (at company expense), but the light plane manufacturers had finally gotten their chance to help the war effort by building thousands of liaison airplanes, trainers, and training gliders.

In the summer of 1940, Lt. James Watson III, called Piper Aircraft and discussed the Artillery's position on the use of the light plane to adjust fire. Lt. Watson advised Piper that the Army was to conduct maneuvers at Camp Beauregard, Louisiana and asked for light aircraft to observe artillery fire. This marked the Army's first contact with Piper. Tom Case of Piper flew a J-3 Cub to Camp Beauregard on August 12, 1940. In Piper's first demonstration for the Army, Case operated the Cub from a dirt road and flew Lt. Watson and others as observers.

Interest in light planes was increasing throughout the Army. General Adna Chaffe, father of the Armored Forces, called Piper on February 9, 1941 and discussed the possibility of having light planes brought to Fort Knox, Kentucky to evaluate his ideas on directing columns of armor from the air. He was intensely interested in adjusting heavy cannon fire from tanks. General Chaffe was delighted with the results from the demonstrations.

General Horace Whittaker, CO of the 45th Infantry Division, also expressed an interest in the light plane. At his request, Tom Case flew to Texas in the same J-3 Cub that he used at Fort Knox. General Whittaker informed General Robert Danford, Chief of Field Artillery, who was a dedicated advocate of the light plane. In a few months, General Danford was to play a key role in the birth of Army Aviation. On April 13, 1941, Case installed a radio in the Cub. The radio was not designed for the Cub, but it did allow two-way voice communication with the Generals.

Henry Wann of Piper Aircraft, telephoned Fort Lewis, Washington to arrange for a visit. He was connected to a Lieutenant Colonel who was interested in Wann's demonstration, especially for artillery fire adjustment. The Colonel added that he had a pilot's license and was well aware of the light plane's abilities. He told Wann his name—Dwight D. Eisenhower.

Eisenhower later went to the war games in the Louisiana Maneuvers.

Cavalry officers at Fort Riley, Kansas witnessed demonstrations of the J-3 Cub on June 12 through June 14, and also became interested in it. On June 18, 1941, some Piper employees took four J-3s to Manchester, Tennessee where they competed against Army Air Forces O-47s in the Tennessee Army maneuvers. This event is especially notable. During these maneuvers the Pipers used by the Army were tagged with the nickname "Grasshoppers" because of their comings and goings.

The light plane's demonstrations were considered a complete success and the Army requested permission to purchase 20 such aircraft. The request was disapproved by the War Department, though. However, Lt. Col. Eisenhower arranged to have the pilots and planes placed on a per diem rental and expense basis. Previously, the government had not paid anything for these demonstrations. In Louisiana, the pilots flew 12 light planes from 12 to 14 hours per day in the Third Army portion of the maneuvers which ran from August 11 through 30, 1941. They continued operating in the same area during the combined Second and Third Army maneuvers from September 1 through 30, 1941. Eisenhower continued to show the same enthusiasm for the airplanes. The successes of the light plane in the Army Maneuvers are shown in that the 12 light planes flew 400,000 miles and over 3,000 missions in operations from June to October of 1941. One plane was lost, but not in the line of duty. However, during the same operations the Air Corps lost 11 O-47s.

The J-3 Cubs were painted yellow—their normal color. In the course of the Louisiana maneuvers, most of the grasshoppers were painted in camouflage schemes—i.e.: olive drab over light gray. During operations when grasshoppers got low on fuel, they simply landed on a highway and refueled at a local filling station. A Cub pilot touched down at this lonely looking gas station expecting to see the local neighborhood turn out and welcome him as a novelty, only to have the attendant tell him that two other grasshoppers had been in that morning and that in the last few days more gas had been sold to airplanes than to automobiles.

While flying a mission, one grasshopper was jumped by an "enemy" P-40. The grasshopper pilot, seeing the 350 MPH Curtis fighter diving down, immediately looked around and spotted a small clearing where he set the lightplane down and taxied beneath some trees. After the grasshopper pilot watched as the P-40 quit looking and left the area, the lightplane pilot took off and resumed his mission.

One of the problems that turned up during the Army war games was the difficulty in keeping the big O-47s active. Very few mechanics were available to service the aircraft and the utility of the O-47 suffered, even though they had to be based at larger fields. The Army found out that almost any motorpool mechanic could keep an L-2, L-3, or L-4 in the air! The utter simplicity of these 65 HP, two-place aircraft was exactly what the Army Ground Forces wanted. They were light, easy to maintain and repair in the field, no electrical systems and fixed wooden propellers. A couple of Army mechanics could change an engine off of the tailgate of a six-by-six truck in just a couple of hours under any and all adverse conditions during battle! And they did so many, many times in the next few years! Operating on roads, unprepared areas, and from small clearings, was sufficiently impressive for the Army to order four test models of each design. The Taylorcraft became the YO-57, the Aeronca the YO-58,

The Curtis 0-52 Owl was an all metal, up-to-date aircraft, with a powerful radial engine, retractable landing gear, and good flying characteristics, but it is not what was needed by the Army. This factory fresh Owl awaits delivery in the winter of 1940 Buffalo, New York. They were quickly relegated to the Air Guard. (NASM)

the Piper the YO-59, and were collectively called "Grasshoppers." The Army did away with the O for observation designation and replaced it with L for liaison in April of 1942. The Stinson O-49 became the L-1, the Taylorcraft O-57 became the L-2, the Aeronca O-58 became the L-3, and the Piper O-59 became the L-4.

Finally the War Department ordered some light planes for the Army. The battle now became one. Not of types of airplanes, but of who would control them. The AAF staff felt they should control all aviation, while the ground forces staff felt they should have control of aviation units working directly within their units. At the working level, the AAF crews of the observation squadrons felt they were too well trained for the lightplanes, and they were more than willing to give the planes to the ground forces or anyone else if it meant they could be transferred to fighter or bomber assignments.

The AAF did very little to promote close cooperation with the Army Ground Forces (AGF). That is why the AGF began to press so hard for its own light aircraft for artillery spotting, courier duties, etc., but such moves were fiercely resisted by the AAF.

The six months following Pearl Harbor were ones of trial where the AAF continued to operate lightplane equipped observation squadrons, but they also loaned 24 Piper O-59s to the ground forces to establish flight training for field artillery personnel at Fort Sill, Oklahoma. This first class consisted of 14 officers and 21 enlisted men who already had CAA pilot's certificates. These men spent six weeks in training and then the graduates and aircraft were attached to the 2nd Infantry Division and the 13th Field Artillery Brigade for tactical exercises.

Finally on June 6, 1942, the War Department officially established organic aviation with the Army Ground Forces, by over-ruling the complaints of the Army Air Forces. Army Aviation had finally come of age.

The War Department directive called for two pilots and one mechanic for each field artillery battalion. Two were placed in each divisional field artillery headquarters. Two were assigned to each field artillery brigade or group headquarters. This required 10 planes in each infantry division which contained four field artillery battalions, six and eventually eight in each armored division, which contained three artillery battalions; and an artillery headquarters. In the field artillery brigade, the number of aircraft varied with the number of battalions in it.

Army Aviation training was ready for business by the end of July and consisted mostly of the members of the test group. In July of 1942, volunteers with civilian pilot ratings were requested to attend the tactical flight course. The 19 students in Class One reported to Fort Sill on August 1, and after preliminary orientation, tactical flight training commenced on August 3 and lasted until September 18. The course, which was later lengthened, used the Piper L-4, the Taylorcraft L-2B and the Aeronca L-3C. Post Field at Fort Sill was turned over to the Army Ground Forces by the Air Corps and several small auxiliary fields were built.

During the early war years, a number of civilians were recruited for the air training department by air shows which were put on at surrounding communities. This aroused a great deal of interest and, along with the recruiting slogan, "that you're better off flying than digging a hole," resulted in a large number of applications. Students received about 15 hours of dual and solo time. Then they were given about 28 hours of flying in and out of small fields, taking off and landing on roads and over obstructions. Towards the end of the course they were given six half-days of instruction as observers. Students also received 12 half-days of ground instruction on navigation and meteorology, 27 half-days on maintenance and repair of airplanes and engines and 3 half-days on tactical employment of organic air observation. All pilots were issued a kit of hand tools and did the maintenance on the aircraft that they flew. When they graduated, they became sergeants, and were reassigned to an operational unit.

Original plans called for 80 percent of the field artillery pilots to be enlisted men. The 20 percent officer pilots were to provide supervision. The plans did not work mainly because the enlisted men who were able to perform an acceptable job as liaison aviators were usually officer candidate material. Consequently, enlisted pilots generally left troop units for OCS shortly after reporting for duty. The War Department decided for enlisted personnel to attend OCS before going to flight school. On April 20, 1943, enlisted men ceased to be eligible for liaison pilot training.

The highly successful employment of Army Aviation in combat resulted in numerous requests for light organic aviation from branches other than field artillery. Therefore, liaison aircraft were effectively employed in such missions as courier and liaison operations, photographic and visual reconnaissance, column control, emergency resupply, and evacuation of wounded.

They were called "grasshoppers," "spotter planes," "Maytag Messerschmitts," "L-Birds" and a variety of other affectionate names. They were used by armed forces all over the world and have served their countries diligently through all conflicts since then. Many of these proud "warbirds" can still be seen at airshows, static displays, and fly-ins worldwide.

CHAPTER TWO

Stinson O-49 / L-1

In January of 1912, a young teenage girl named Katherine Stinson took her first airplane ride. Her pilot was the great Tony Jannus. She loved it, and continued flying. She became the fourth woman pilot in the United States. By 1913, she and Ruth Law were the leading female pilots, which were extremely rare at that time. She became very popular, so Katherine and her mother incorporated the Stinson Aviation Company in April of 1913 in Hot Springs, Arkansas.

Katherine's brother, Eddie joined them. Matty Laird taught Eddie to fly. By this time war clouds were gathering in Europe where aviation had taken enormous strides forward. The need for European pilots was great, especially for the British Royal Flying Corps (RFC.) Canada wanted to help, but they had no flying schools, so they asked Stinson to train some Canadian pilots for the RFC. Stinson graduated her first class of five Canadians in November of 1915 using Wright B trainers.

Stinson bought more aircraft for training from Grover Leoning. Late in 1916, the commander of the 1st Aero Squadron, Captain Benjamin Foulois, hired Eddie Stinson to teach new students to fly. Eddie basically invented the spin recovery maneuver. Capt. Foulois wanted the new "stunt" taught to his students. The flying school was very busy during World War I.

Katherine then expanded and started an air mail route from Chicago to New York in May of 1918. In July of 1918, she flew air mail to Calgary, Edmonton, Canada to do the first air mail in Canada. Finally in 1928, Katherine married Mike Otero, a World War I aviator. She never flew again, and became a housewife.

In Atlantic City, New Jersey, while flying at a airshow, a timid young lady who had always been fearful of heights, took her first ride with Eddie Stinson, very reluctantly. But when Stinson looped the Jenny that they were flying in, Ruth Nichols fear vanished. She was soon flying her own plane. Later Ruth Nichols

One of the three competitors for the "Storch-like" liaison aircraft contract, was the Ryan Y0-51. It was a two-place STOL aircraft with a Pratt & Whitney R-985 engine of 450 HP. The span was an amazing 52 feet. It had a gross weight of only 4206 pounds. As evident here in this photograph, the "Dragonfly" has full-span slats and flaps for very low speed handling. Three were built. They were 40-703 through 705. (NASM)

The Ryan Y0-51 Dragonfly was based on the German Fielscher Fi-156 Storch (Stork), as is clearly noticeable here at Ryan's San Diego, California factory. The two seat, open cockpit was beautifully built, but it had no room for additional equipment or growth. (NASM)

became the first woman airline pilot.

In 1921, Eddie Stinson bought a Junkers, a large all metal cabin monoplane built in Germany. Eddie wanted to demonstrate its potential, so on November 21, 1921, he flew non-stop Chicago to New York City with four passengers. That was the first commercial flight between the two cities. In 1922 Stinson moved to Detroit to establish his charter operations. Stinson saw a need for a charter-type of an aircraft. So he hired a man to design one. Stinson wanted a cabin heater, wheel brakes, and an electric starter. Taken separately, such features were not unique. Collectively, they had yet to appear on a single aircraft. The resulting airplane was the Stinson Detroiter, which first flew on January 25, 1926.

In March, Stinson received a call from Horace Dodge, the automobile magnate. He wanted to fly to Washington, D. C. immediately. Stinson said he would fly him, only if he purchased a Detroiter for his future needs. Thus the Stinson Detroiter became one of the first corporate aircraft. It also helped the start-up of some airlines like Northwest Airways, and Florida Airways. Stinson began building the Detroiter in numbers.

In April of 1929, Stinson moved his factory to Wayne, Michigan, a suburb of Detroit. Stinson produced 121 aircraft in 1929 to become the countries third largest aircraft manufacturer. This success attracted many investors, including E. L. Cord, owner of the Cord, Duesenberg, and Auburn automobiles, Lycoming Motors, and other corporations. So Cord bought a controlling interest in Stinson Aircraft.

Stinson started making larger aircraft like the Stinson SM-6000 tri-motor airliner. The airliner seated 11 passengers. Full loaded, it would take-off in 700 feet and had a landing roll of only 400 feet. It was considered to be the finest airliner of its time. 35 were built. So Cord asked Stinson to start an airline to utilize the new tri-motor airliner. They founded Century Airlines, and Century Pacific Airlines. In 1933 Cord sold the airlines to Aviation Corporation, a holding company, which became American Airlines. American used the Stinson tri-motors and Stinson also sold some to another small airline just getting started named Delta Airlines. But the depression was in full swing, so, in order to sell more airplanes, Stinson started work on smaller airplanes. The result was one of the finest personal aircraft—the Stinson Reliant. More on that aircraft later.

In September of 1938 at the National Air Races in Cleveland, the German Luftwaffe was invited to display some aircraft. The Germans, wanting to show off their much-vaunted Luftwaffe, wanted to display their superiority of the Fieseler Fi-156 Storch, the German word for stork. The Storch was the first light STOL aircraft designed specifically for the Army liaison role. Its appearance had tremendous and very long-lasting effect on the U.S. military. Pilot Emil Kroph could make the airplane almost hover in a 30 MPH wind, with full control, and repeated take-off and landing almost vertically. Nothing like the Storch had previously been seen in America.

The U.S. Army wanted its own Storch, so they put out a request for proposals to manufacturers. Twelve

The second of the three competitors for the "Storch-like" liaison aircraft contract, was the Bellanca Y0-50. It was two-place STOL aircraft with a Ranger V-770 engine of 420 HP. It has a wing span of 34 feet, 2 inches, and a length of 21 feet, 3 inches. It had a range of 410 miles. Three were built. They were 40-741 through 743. They had very large flaps, and full-span slots in the leading edge of the wing. This is the first one built—40-741. (NASM)

submitted designs. Stinson's proposal, the Model 74, closely followed the Storch formula. It employed full-span Handley-Page automatic slats and slotted flaps. The airframe was a conventional steel-tube structure, and fabric-covered. Of the three contract winners, only Stinson received a production order. The runners-up were the Bellanca YO-50, and the Ryan YO-51. They were awarded orders for an experimental model only to be built. The Stinson contract, valued at $1,500,000, was for 142 aircraft. The Stinson O-49 won the competition because it was less complex and cheaper to build.

The Stinson Model 74, or YO-49 was completed, but the Wayne, Michigan aircraft factory was in full production of the Reliant, so Cord bought a factory in Nashville, Tennessee. First flight was in Nashville on July 15, 1940. It proved to be an amazing airplane. Test pilot Al Schramm demonstrated the YO-49 capabilities by flying in and out of a 200 feet circle. It was a bad landing if the roll-out was more than ten yards. With a brisk headwind, it would even fly backwards. The YO-49 was an outstanding performer. It was the Army's first STOL-type liaison aircraft. The YO-49 began military service as the O-49 Vigilant in September of 1940.

Stinson received a second production contract for 182 more O-49s called the O-49A. All O-49s/L-1s were produced in Nashville, Tennessee. The contract number issued was W535-AC-17910 by the War Department. In August of 1940, Cord sold his Stinson Aircraft division to Vultee Aircraft through a stock transfer arranged by Aviation Corporation (Avco), the parent company. Avco also owned Lycoming Motors and therefore, Stinsons were powered by Lycoming engines. Shortly thereafter, Vultee merged with Consolidated Aircraft to become Consolidated-Vultee or shorted to Convair which became General Dynamics.

The Vigilant, with its high wing and its pronounced dihedral, was a very stable aircraft. The controls were heavy, though, and the ailerons responded a little sluggishly, but the rudder and elevators were aerodynamically balanced perfectly. Nevertheless, it is a jewel to fly. The pilot's visibility in turns is much better than most other high-wing aircraft. There is also a sliding

(Above) ***The winner of the "Storch-like" liaison aircraft competition was the Stinson YO-49 Vigilant. This 0-49 was just delivered to the 111 s' Observation Squadron at Brownwood, Texas in July of 1941. The top of the cowling was painted flat black for anti-glare of the bright Texas sunshine. The full-span slats are shown here. (Tom Hale)***

(Above) ***The 111st Observation Squadron was one of many participants during the Carolina Maneuvers. Shown here is the flight line on November 8, 1941 at Greenville, South Carolina. The Stinson 0-49 in the foreground has already been painted in Olive Drab as have the other types of observation aircraft in the background. In the background are Douglas 0-43s and Curtis 0-52s. (Tom Hale)***

(Below) ***This Stinson 0-49B ambulance plane is located at Moffet Field, California on December 6, 1941. The designation was later changed to L-1. The red cross on the fuselage means it was an ambulance plane, not a participant in the recently completed Louisiana War Games and the Carolina Maneuvers. The upper area behind the rear door has been modified to carry the patient on a stretcher. (NASM)***

The 111st Observation Squadron used motorcycles with side cars for flight line transportation. The motorcycle was equipped with a siren on the left handle bar. The 0-49 had just been delivered in July of 1941 at Brownsville, Texas airport. A ground crew member is handing the pilot some papers just prior to a flight. (Tom Hale)

(Above) ***A Stinson 0-49 Vigilant flies over the Tennessee countryside in 1941. The fifty-one feet wing span had full-span slats, and full-span trailing edge flaps allowed the 0-49 to fly at very low speeds. The top part of the cockpit was all glass, and the side were canted outward for visibility straight down. All of the glass made for some very warm cockpits. Therefore, the door windows were usually open in flight for cooling. (NASM)***

(Below) ***A waterspout is seen just above this 0-49 at Gulfport, Mississippi on August 1, 1941. The 0-49 had already been painted for the Louisiana War Games in Olive Drab as had the 0-49 barely visible in front of the fuel tanker. The aircraft were in the area for the war games. (Minnesota Air Guard Museum)***

skylight window overhead, which may be opened in flight. The full-length slots on the leading edge of the wings, allowed the Vigilant to virtually hover above the tree tops over troops or armor units. It could fly at a speed substantially less than an automobile could travel on a city street and still maintain its altitude. The Vigilant was also used later for mapping and reconnaissance roles.

Although the Vigilant was designed solely for the role of a two-seat army liaison and observation landplane, it did gain the distinction of becoming one of the very few amphibious float seaplanes to serve during World War II. The Edo Aircraft Corporation had designed special amphibious float gear for the Vigilant. Known as the Model 77 amphibious gear, this combined two long single-step floats each of which embodied retractable nose gear and main wheels. This gear was fitted to two ambulance conversions of the O-49/L-1, these being redesignated L-1E, and to one ambulance conversion of the L-1A, this becoming the L-1F. The principle difference between the two models being the longer fuselage length of the L-1F.

(Below) ***A close up photograph of the nose section of camouflaged Stinson 0-49 shows details of the cowlings, and numerous support struts in the cockpit area. The full-span slats are extended. The cowling had no cooling flaps. (Tom Hale)***

Stinson 0-49, number 13 of the 154th Observation Squadron (formally Arkansas National Guard), is shown here during the Louisiana War Games in September of 1941. The full-span flaps are down as well as the full-span slats. No serial numbers were carried on the tail, but under the wings the numbers 154013 indicate the 154th Observation Squadron, aircraft number 13. (Tom Hale)

When the O-49 was delivered, many of the pilots simply would not believe that "slower is better" for observation missions. Some even felt that the O-49 was a step backwards. Most military pilots believed that the faster a plane flew the better it was. The Army Air Corps listened to the complaints from its observation pilots and reconsidered its choice of aircraft. Ignoring the pleas of the ground forces for slower, lighter observation aircraft, the Air Corps ordered no more Vigilants and ordered the Curtis O-52 Owl to potentially replace the O-49. The new Owl was a high-wing, all-metal craft with retractable landing gear. Powered by a 600 HP Pratt & Whitney R-1340 engine with a top speed of 208 MPH, it had a 40 feet, 9 inch wing span, a weight of 4,231 pounds empty, and 5,344 pounds at maximum weight. The Owl was a total waste of time and effort. It just did not work for what it was designed for. But, the Vigilant was vital during the war, and served in all theatres of operations.

It served as an ambulance, aerial observation post, artillery fire control, supply craft, and many other vital uses. The Vigilant held only 67 gallons of gasoline. Total production of the O-49/L-1 was 352 of which 33 went to the British under Lend-Lease. They served in Tunisia, Sicily, and Italy in 1943 and 1944 with the RAF. In addition, one Vigilant was built for the U.S. Navy. The Bureau of Aeronautics number was 09799 and designated the GQ-1.

Although relatively large and complex, the Stinson L-1 proved difficult to maintain in the field with only a minimum of ground equipment. It also had an inherently weak landing gear, and it also required a lot of aviation gasoline, which was not always readily available in the field. Consequently, despite its excellent short field performance, only a limited production run ensued.

The Vigilant was a real work-horse. It was tricky to land in a cross-wind because of the dihedral of the wings. Because of its size and weight, it was a mechanics nightmare. Just to move it on its long spindley landing gear required six to eight strong men. To clean the windshield or check the oil required hanging by one hand and working with the other. Just to change a tire meant the use of a two-ton jack. When a propeller or an

Stinson 0-49, number 12 of the 22nd Observation Squadron, during the Louisiana War Games, in September of 1941, is landing with the flaps down. The aircraft number is on the cowling and also on the tail above the number 22 and the letter "O" for observation. The under-surfaces of the wings, fuselage, and horizontal stabilizers are all painted gray camouflage. (Tom Hale)

Stinson 0-49, number 12 of the 22nd Observation Squadron, during the Louisiana War Games, in September of 1941, is flying above the Louisiana countryside during the war games. On top of the left wing are the number 22012, meaning the 22nd Observation Squadron, aircraft number 12. (Tom Hale)

Another in-flight photograph of aircraft number 12 of the 22nd Observation Squadron, during the Louisiana War Games in September of 1941, shows a large tail surface that is needed for slow speed maneuvering. (Tom Hale)

Aircraft number 12 of the 22nd Observation Squadron, displays slow speed flight during the Louisiana War Games during September of 1941. When the flaps are lowered, the ailerons also are lowered automatically, giving the aircraft a full-span flap area. (Tom Hale)

Two flight crew members congratulate each other after another successful flight in a Stinson 0-49. Note the angled outward glass and windows on the fuselage side of the Vigilant. (Minnesota Air Guard Museum)

engine change was needed, special tools and hoist equipment had to be used.

Numerous L-1s were used in Alaska during World War II for search and rescue missions along the routes used by the ferry pilots flying P-39s etc. to Siberia for the Russian Air Force. Following the war, several surplus L-1s were converted to float planes for use in the Alaska "bush."

As an ambulance, it could take out 2 or 3 casualties at one time, which the Army found out in Burma with

A Stinson L-1 and an Stinson L-1E amphibian at Myogan Airfield in Burma, share the flightline with a wrecked C-47 in the background. There were only seven L-lEs built. They were ambulance interiors with two Edo floats. The float-equipped L- l appears to have a U S Navy-type of camouflage on it. (USAF)

the 1st Air Commando Group. They were evacuating wounded personnel in support for General Stillwell, Merrill's Marauders, and Chinese and British troops. The 100 pilots and 75 L-1s helped fly out over 1,000 casualties. The 1st ACG lost only 5 pilots, two of them strafed by the Japanese on takeoff.

Performance of the O-49/L-1 was legendary. Wallace "Wally " Thomas was stationed in Hawaii in 1941 flying the Vigilant from Bellows Field on the north side of the island of Oahu. Wally always read the local Honolulu newspapers each morning and checking the arrival dates and times of the sea going passenger and cruise ships sailing from the states. He would fly out in his O-49 to meet the ship some 50 or 60 miles out at sea. Once over the ship, he would slow the O-49 down to almost stall speed, and "hover" over the fantail of the ship, generally over the swimming pool. He would wave at the girls and, of course, they would wave back. Wally would make gestures to indicate the message "I will meet you on the dock." After getting an affirmative return gesture from a girl or two. Wally would then fly back to Bellows Field, jump into his car, rushed to his quarters, get cleaned-up into his best "meet-you-on-the-dock" clothes, buy a Lei of Hawaiian flowers and meet his shipboard date at the dock. He says the

Mechanics change the engine (Lycoming R-680-9) of an Stinson L- l in the field - probably Burma, in 1943. The Stinson L-l was fairly difficult to work on, requiring lots of "extra hands" for maintenance. (USAF)

The flightline at Greenville, South Carolina on November 8, 1941, shows a Stinson 0-49 on the left. In the middle are two Curtis 0-52 Owls, and the rest on the right are Douglas 0-43s. All aircraft have by now been painted Olive Drab. (Tom Hale)

arrangement worked real well for him until the morning of December 7, 1941.

A small number of Stinson L-1s arrived in England during 1943 and early 1944, but very few were immediately assigned to AAF units. Instead, they were mostly utilized as stretcher-equipped ambulance aircraft, and were held in storage. At least two were converted to normal seating configuration for use by General Eisenhower. A few L-1s were painted an overall aluminum or silver finish in early 1945.

STINSON O-49/L-1 Vigilant

Wing span—50feet, 11 inches
Length—34 feet, 3 inches
Height—10 feet, 2 inches
Wing area—329 square feet
Empty weight—2,670 pounds
Gross weight—3,400 pounds
Engine—Lycoming R-680-9 with 295 HP
Crew—one or two
Maximum speed—122 MPH
Cruise speed—108 MPH
Stalling speed—31 MPH
Climb—1100 feet per minute
Ceiling—20,000 feet
Range—350 miles

PRODUCTION OF THE STINSON O-49/ L-1 VIGILANT, MODEL 74

L-1-ST ex O-49
L-1A-ST ex O-49A
L-1B-ST ex O-49B

L-1C-ST An L-1A-ST was modified with a loading hatch in the upper fuselage decking and cabin provision for a stretcher as the L-1C-ST. It was later converted to an L-1F-ST. Eventually 113 L-1C conversions were completed.

L-1D-ST A total of 21 L-1A-STs were converted for glider pick-up training.

L-1E-ST Seven L-1A-STs with ambulance interiors and twin Edo floats with retractable nose and main wheels.

L-1F-ST The L-1C-ST conversion fitted with Edo floats. An additional 4 L-1A-STs were reported to have been similarly converted.

CQ-1 One O-49A was built for the U.S. Navy. It was BuNo. 09799.

CQ-2 Designation given to a small number of L-1s converted for remote control of targets.

O-49 Initial production model, with a 295 HP R-680-9 and pilot and observer in tandem. 142 were built. Serial numbers were 40-192 through -291 and 40-3101 through -3142.

O-49A As an O-49, but with a 13-inch fuselage extension and higher gross weight. 182 were built. Serial numbers were 41-18900 through -19081.

O-49B Four O-49s that were adapted for ambulance duties.

RAF The RAF called their version the Vigilant also.

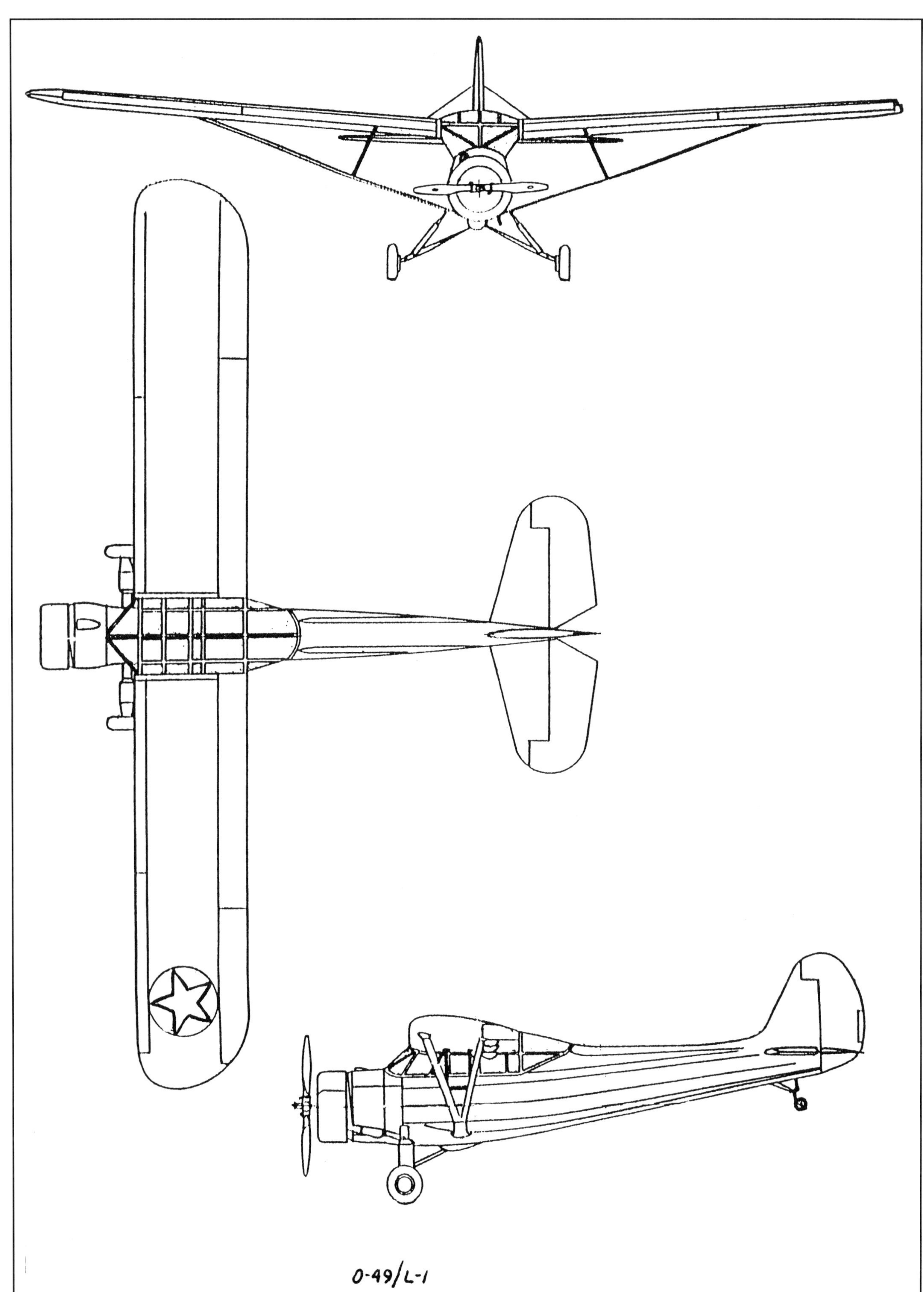
0-49/L-1

CHAPTER THREE

Taylorcraft O-57 / L-2 Grasshopper

The Taylorcraft O-57/L-2 was designed and built by the man who originally designed and built the E-2 Taylor Cub, which later became the Piper Cub and the O-59/L-4 Grasshopper. It was in 1930 that C. Gilbert Taylor, and his brother organized the Taylor Aircraft Corporation at Bradford, Pennsylvania.

Actually the Taylorcraft story begins in 1935 when C. Gilbert Taylor sold his share of the Taylor Aircraft Company to his other partner, William T. Piper, who promptly changed the name of the company to the Piper Aircraft Company. William Piper was an investor who financed the very successful "Taylor Cub." The Cub was a tandem two-seat, single engine, high-wing monoplane, which prospered because of its economically low cost of operation and maintenance and low purchase price, which was a major factor during the 1930s depression era. Taylor felt that the Taylor Cub, with a few changes, could be made more comfortable with entry doors and could possibly be made to go faster with a re-designed wing. The difference in opinions between Taylor and Piper, plus other differences, led to the parting of their partnership. Piper kept company, the Cub and all of the manufacturing rights which, of course, led to the infamous Piper Cub family of aircraft.

Taylor was not going to stop building airplanes. So, he formed the Taylor Aircraft Company, and began design and production in a shop in Butler, Pennsylvania. It was in this shop that the first Taylorcraft Model A was built.

Taylor used the basic Cub design, streamlined it, placed the seats side-by-side, and used a wheel instead of a stick for control. The T-Craft used the 40 horsepower, Continental four-cylinder, air-cooled engine, which was the same one Taylor had used in the Cub. The Model A could fly a few miles per hour faster than the Cub. The Cub and the new Taylorcraft Model A bore a distinct family resemblance—in fact they were quite similar, and to the untrained eye, could have been the same model or the same type of airplane.

Taylor's Model A became an immediate success. It was such a success that the factory would have to be expanded. However, with the depression in full swing, there was no extra money to make such an expansion. But the city of Alliance, Ohio heard about the potential expansion, and offered Taylor a plant rent-free. It was an offer that Taylor could not refuse. So, the factory was moved. By August of 1937, the 200th Taylorcraft Model A had been built and sold. Production in 1938 reached 75 units per month.

The Taylorcraft Model B came out in late 1938 with the 50 HP Continental engine which was later upgraded to 65 HP.

Taylorcraft 0-57 actually was a tandem-seat trainer developed for the Civilian Pilot Training Program (CPTP). This very early 0-57 displays the standard U S Army insignias and color scheme of Olive Drab. The resemblance to the Piper Cub is very close, and sometimes very difficult to tell apart from a distance. (U S Army Aviation Museum)

This Taylorcraft 0-57/L-2, number 127, at Fort Sill, Oklahoma in 1942, was the first fatality for liaison aircraft at the artillery spotting school. (U S Army Aviation Museum)

With the war obviously on the horizon, Taylorcraft designed and built a trainer version, and it was this version that became the O-57 and later the L-2 by the Army. Though Piper captured the lion's share of the market with the Cub, there was a need for more trainers. Aeronca and Taylorcraft hastily went into production to build tandem-seat trainers. Taylor's next design was the Model D, and it was a case of using what you have and going on from there. Model B wings and the tail group were fitted onto a fuselage. Tandem seating extended the fuselage 9 inches in length.

The O-57/L-2 was designed as a "bare bones" Army trainer and not targeted for the civilian market. Used as a trainer it was designed to be, the Model DC-65 tandem trainer became a real workhorse.

The Aeronca and Piper designs retained their origi-

The interior of the Taylorcraft L-2 was very spartan. Just two canvas-covered seats, a few basic instruments, and a joystick - that was about it. The large side windows could open for cooling in the air or on the ground. (SMR)

The visibility from the cockpit was tremendous! Yes, there were less than ten instruments to monitor. The low speed made it very easy to pickup details on the ground - anything faster would have been missed because of the higher speed. (SMR)

nal fuselage contours and merely made the area immediately behind the wing transparent. Taylorcraft chose to make more extensive changes. It cut off the superstructure of the upper fuselage from the trailing-edge of the wing to the leading-edge of the vertical stabilizer to produce a low, flat deck level with the upper longerons and then extended enlarged rear cabin windows into a streamlined fairing behind the rear seat.

More changes were made to the L-2M, which featured a cowled engine and wing spoilers, similar to those on a glider to allow steep approaches to small landing areas. None of the "Big Three" liaison builders had used flaps on their aircraft. The L-2M was the last L-2 model that Taylorcraft would build.

On February 17, 1942, the War Production Board prohibited the sale of light planes to anyone except to the U.S. Army and Navy. At that same time, the Army glider pilot program was seriously handicapped by a shortage of suitable training gliders and glider schools.

Piper and Aeronca had bolted new noses onto the engine mount points, but Taylorcraft cut the frame back to the wing-strut attachment point, and used a different nose-structure for the glider. The Aeronca training glider became the TG-5, the Taylorcraft became the TG-6, and the Piper became the TG-8. The Army ordered about 250 from each of the manufacturers after evaluating a model of each manufacturer.

This beautifully restored Taylorcraft L-2A carries the standard camouflage scheme from 1943. The yellow tail serial numbers were not added at the factory, but in the field, usually when the aircraft was assigned to a unit. (SMR)

At the war's end, the "Big Three" liaison manufacturers resumed production of pre-war models. Aeronca modernized its tandem L-3 into the post-war Champion 7AC. Piper resumed production of the J-3

The Taylorcraft L-2 made a very cheap and a true warbird. This L-2A shows the modified cabin, and wing trailing edge cut away near the wing root. The L-2A was equipped with the SCR-585 radio. The observer's seat could face to the rear. 476 L-2As were built. (SMR)

Auster AOP, now registered in Great Britain as G-AIBR, was a veteran of the RAF. The only difference now is the color scheme, and the radios and minor military equipment removed at the end of the war. The over-head glass is still readily apparent and gives great visibility. Obtaining parts for the British engine is not a problem in England. (Author)

Cub. But Taylorcraft went back to manufacturing as the pre-war side-by-side model, the BC-12, and dropped the tandem-seat Model D. But that was not the end of the line for the Taylorcraft tandem. Many Army L-2s went into the surplus market as did most of the TG-6 gliders. The TG-6 gliders were useless to the small soaring fraternities, so they were sold to power-plane owners. With the Aeronca and Piper gliders, the conversion to power involved only removing the glider nose, removing or deactivating the spoilers and re-attaching stock engine mounts, cowling and landing gear to obtain a standard license under the original A.T.C. The Taylorcraft glider, because of the cut-away forward fuselage structure, was not too easy to convert and since the factory was not interested in making a conversion, about 25 or 30 small shops and individuals undertook the conversion work on their own. The surplus L-2s could be licensed under their original A.T.C.

This Auster AOP was purchased as war surplus after World War II, and registered in Great Britain. In order to de-militarize an AOP, all you did was pull out some radios and minor military equipment, and you had yourself an instant civil aircraft. G-AJDW is shown here in 1964, and the only change has been a new paint job and registration. (Author)

Some were changed or "civilianized" and some were rebuilt and some were just repainted.

In 1943, the U.S. Navy followed the Army's lead in abandoning sailplane-type gliders for primary and familiarization training and adopted modified liaison-type from which the 65 HP Continental engines had been removed and replaced by an extra seat in the nose to maintain balance. The Navy bought 35 Army Taylorcraft TG-6s, 10 as the XLNT-1 and 25 as the LNT-1. These had sinking rates and speeds and glide ratios more compatible with the cargo-type gliders the pilots were eventually to fly. Shortly thereafter, the Navy pulled out of the glider programs altogether.

Over the years, a number of American designed aircraft have been licensed to foreign manufacturers for production and sales. One of the best known examples of pre-World War II years was the Taylorcraft and in the case of the T-Craft, a popular nickname of the Taylorcraft airplanes, was licensed to the Taylorcraft Aeroplanes Limited formed at Turmaston, Leicester, England in 1938. Taylorcraft Aeroplanes Limited had completed 22 Model Cs by the summer of 1939 when the beginning of WWII ended all civil aircraft production.

The British firm converted all remaining unassembled Model C airframes with engine mounts to take the popular British Cirrus Minor four-cylinder inverted air-cooled engines. These engines were used in the early models, designated as the Auster I and the Auster II's "mounted" the American Lycoming O-290, 130 HP engine. But to avoid the risk of importing the American engines in wartime, the RAF used a British engine, the 130 HP De Havilland Gipsy Major engine and produced 467 Auster IIIs, the most popular WWII British liaison aircraft.

Another one of the U.S. Navy's secret projects during the war was the Gliding Bomb Project and assigned the designation LBT-1. Few people knew that a super-secret Taylorcraft glider was designed and built or modified to deliver the Atomic Bomb! Al Barber was the test pilot on this GLOMB—(glider/bomb) project. The Glomb concept was that a glider be built that could be flown into the target area by a remote controlled aircraft with the guidance being a television camera in the nose of the Glomb sending back to a screen in the mother aircraft where the remote control "pilot" sat guiding the gliding bomb onto the target. This was a very early version of the modern-day "smart bombs." Of course, we now know that the whole idea was to get the mother ship away from the target so there would be no damage from the extreme shock created by the Atomic bomb. A TG-6 could have been the ship to carry the bomb to Japan or Germany. Instead they found that a B-29 at extreme high altitude could get away from the blast successfully. Both Piper and Taylorcraft built a Glomb.

The Glomb was tested originally with a pilot on board and flown many hours before the electronic guidance equipment was installed. A similar project was going on at the same time with a B-24 being loaded with high explosives and then taken off with a small crew onboard who then armed the impact switches and bailed out allowing the mother ship to follow and guide it to the target. Joe Kennedy, brother of the future President of the United States, John F. Kennedy, was killed in this type of aircraft over England when the aircraft blew up during the arming procedure prior to bail out.

TAYLOR CRAFT O-57/L-2 GRASSHOPPER, MODEL D TWO-SEATER

L-2-TA ex O-57-TA

L-2A-TA ex O-57A-TA

L-2B-TA Same as L-2A-TA but with modified equipment for artillery spotting. It has an 65 HP O-170-3 engine. 490 were built. Serial numbers were 43-1 though 43-490.

L-2C-TA 13 impressed Model DC-65 with the Continental A-65-8 of 65 HP with two seats in tandem. Serial numbers were 43-2800, 43-2802 through -2806, 43-2868 through -2873, and 43-2901.

L-2D-TA One impressed Model DC-65 with 65 HP O-145-BZ engine, with two seats in tandem. Serial number was 43-2902.

L-2E-TA Ten impressed Model DF-65 with a 65 HP Franklin 4AC-150 engine with two seats in tandem. Serial numbers were 43-2859, -2861, -2867, -2890 through -2892, and -2903 through -2906.

L-2F-TA Seven impressed Model BL-65, originally given the designation UC-95-TA. The engine was a 65 HP 0-145-B1. It had two side-by-side seats. Serial numbers were 42-79556, 43-2881 through -2883, -2889, -2993, and -2908.

L-2G-TA Two impressed Model BFT-65s with a 65 HP Franklin 4AC-150 engine. They had tandem seats. Serial numbers were 43-2888 and -2907.

L-2H-TA Nine impressed Model BC12-65s with two side-by-side seats. The engine was a 65 HP Continental A-65-7. Serial numbers were 43-2874, -2879, -2880, -2883 though -2886, -2895 through -2897, and -2900.

L-2J-TA Five impressed Model BLI2-65 which was the same as the L-2H-TA, but with a 65 HP O-145-BI engine. Serial numbers were 43-2875 through -2877, and—2898 and -2907.

L-2K-TA Four impressed Model BF12-65 which was the same as the L-2H-TA, but with a 65 HP Franklin 4AC-150 engine. Serial numbers were 43-2878, -2884, -2887, and -2894.

L-2L-TA One impressed Model BF50 with two side-by-side seats with a 50 HP Franklin 4AC-150 engine. The serial number was 42-79559.

L-2M-TA Same as the L-2A-TA with a close-fitting engine cowling and wing spoilers. 900 were built. Serial numbers were 43-25854 through -26753.

UC-95-TA One Taylorcraft BL-65 (serial number 2495,) registered in Panama to an American citizen named R. D. Maynard. It was impressed as the only UC-95 with the serial number 42-79556. It was re-registered as the L-2F-TA and withdrawn from use in December of 1944.

YO-57-TA Four Model Ds for evaluation with a 65 HP YO-170-3 engine. Serial numbers were 42-452 through -455.

O-57-TA Same as the YO-57, but with small changes and a 65 HP O-170-3 engine. Seventy were built. Serial numbers were 42-7773 through -7792, and 43-2859 through -2908.

O-57A-TA Same as the O-57, but with a modified cabin, wing trailing edge cut away near the wing root for the military SCR-585 radio. The observer's seat could face aft. 336 were built with the serial numbers 42-15073 through -15158 and 35825 through -36074. An additional 140 were ordered and built with the serial numbers 42-38498 through -38531, and 43-25754 through -25853.

TG-6-TA Model ST100 three-seat training glider version of the L-2 with enlarged fin area, wing spoilers, and a simplified landing gear. 250 production models were built. Serial numbers were 42-58561 through -58810. One was rebuilt as the XTG-33-TA. Three (43-12496 through -12498) were ordered for delivery to the U.S. Navy as the XLNT-1. Bureau of Aeronautics were 36428 through 36430. Seven were transferred to the U.S. Navy as Bu 67800 through 67806.

XTG-33-TA Two TG-6-TA was extensively rebuilt in 1945 with a prone station for the pilot as the XTG-33-TA. It did not work at all.

XLNT-1 U.S. Navy version of the TG-6-TA, ten of which were obtained from the USAAF as the XLNT-1. The Bu numbers were 36428 through 36430, and ex- 43-10491 through 43-10498 which were Bu numbers 67800 through 67806.

LNT-1 25 production examples were built. Bureau of Aeronautics numbers were 87763 through 87787.

TAYLORCRAFT O-57/L-2 Grasshopper

Wing span = 35 feet, 5 inches
Length—22 feet, 9 inches
Height—8 feet, 0 inches
Wing area—181 square feet
Empty weight—875 pounds
Gross weight—1,300 pounds
Engine— Continental 0-170-3 (A-65-8) of 65 HP
Crew—one or two
Maximum speed—98 MPH
Cruise speed—78 MPH
Climb—350 feet per minute
Ceiling—10,050 feet
Range—230 miles

CHAPTER FOUR

Aeronca O-58 / L-3 Grasshopper

The story of the development of the Aeronca begins with a 12 year old French immigrant named Jean Roche. The young boy developed a passionate love of aviation and became a skilled model builder. He was able to win many awards for the excellent flying characteristics of the models.

Simplicity and functionalism were Roche's keynotes to sound engineering. He recognized that aircraft design is a series of compromises between such factors as range, weight, useful load and fuel load. He kept weight to a minimum as a matter of course and insisted on strict functionality of all parts.

The single wing monoplane was far superior to the two winged biplane and was steadily maintained by Roche. This fact was born out when his light monoplane was able to out perform, on less horsepower, the standard biplanes of the day.

John O. Dorse, an assistant to Roche, volunteered his service and the two man team was better able to come up with a complete, yet simple little airplane to be flown for fun.

The Aeronautical Corporation of America (Aeronca) was formed in November of 1928. Here was a company with assets of over one half million dollars, but no factory, no employees, and no airplane to build. It was decided by the group that the new facility would be based at the Lunken Airport near Cincinnati, Ohio.

After much testing and a few modifications, a deal was made with Roche for the manufacture of his airplane. He was to receive 220 shares of stock in the newly formed company and was to act in as advisory capacity.

A factory-fresh Aeronca L-3 awaits delivery to the U S Army Air Forces in 1943. The Aeronca L-3 was in such demand early in the war, that the Army impressed over 100 civilian versions of the L-3. The USAAF serial numbers were not carried on the tail. However, the manufacturers serial number is. It is written in chalk on the tail - 1657. (NASM)

The first production airplane was to be known as the Aeronca C-2. It was a single place monoplane powered by a 26 HP, two cylinder, air cooled engine developed by the Aeronca itself. The next production model was a modification of the C-2 to be known as the C-3. It seated two people and had a bit more powerful Aeronca two cylinder, 36 HP air cooled engine. Many of the C-3s were built and sold as a very economical dual training aircraft during the depression era. Many of

The prototype of the Aeronca 0-58B, 42-14713, in early 1942 displays its camouflage and the red disc insignia of the U S Army Air Corps. It was delivered under its original 0-58B designation, but changed to L-3B. (NASM)

The seventy-first Aeronca 0-58/L-3 built carried the standard camouflage in early 1942, which was Olive Drab over Neutral Gray. The U S insignia still had the red disc in it. The disc was eliminated on May 15, 1942 to avoid confusion with the Japanese "red meat ball" insignia called the Homiru. (NASM)

today's pilots, including many retired airline pilots, learned to fly during that era, received their dual and solo and built up the required hours to get their commercial, instructor's license and air transport pilots certificates, in the Aeronca C-3. Paying $1.50 an hour for dual instruction, and $1.00 per hour for solo flight time, was a good price back then.

In April of 1938, the Aeronca company introduced the Aeronca Chief, with the newly released Continental Twin Ignition 50 HP engine. About 200 of these the Chief aircraft were built the first year. Next year, in 1939, the Army tested the Aeronca 50-C (50 Hp Chief) as a trainer, but due to its side-by-side cockpit arrangement, turned it down—sticking to its old theory that all training airplanes should have a tandem seating cockpit arrangement. Of course, the military later reversed this thinking, as seen by the very long-lasting, and still operating Cessna T-37.

One of the four Aeronca YO-58s obtained by the U S Army Air Corps in 1941 for testing. The Army was pleased with the aircraft and ordered them in quantity. (NASM)

As the "clouds of war" began to cover the world, the United States began stepping up its flight training program. To be in competition, Aeronca introduced the Aeronca Tandem Trainer. The Aeronca Trainer, simply used the wings and tail of the Chief with tandem fuselage in place of the side-by-side fuselage.

In order to increase sales and to be more competitive with Piper and Taylorcraft, Aeronca refined and modified the trainer into what became known as the Aeronca Defender. From the Defender, came the Aeronca YO-58, then the O-58 and finally the definitive model of the L-3.

A factory-fresh Aeronca 0-58B awaits delivery to a military unit. The B model differed from the A model by having increased window area and other military equipment added. (NASM)

The wing of the Aeronca was covered by cotton cloth and the doped. The L-3 had ailerons only, no flaps or slats or slots for low speed flight. Lots of "glass" made for great visibility in all directions for either the front or back seat. The L-3 was very easy to fly. (Aeronca)

For the 1941 Army maneuvers, Aeronca, Piper, and Taylorcraft virtually forced their airplanes on the Army for testing and trials in Louisiana. These airplanes were accompanied by sharp pilots and company mechanics. Their operations from roads, unprepared areas and small clearings was sufficient for the Army to order four test models of each company's design. The Taylorcraft became the YO-57, the Aeronca was the YO-58, and the Piper was the YO-59. All were collectively given the nickname "Grasshopper" by one General during the maneuvers who observed the small planes landing and taking off from unprepared fields, made the comment "They look just like Grasshoppers in a corn field."

After Pearl Harbor in early 1942, the Army changed the designation from "O" for Observation to "L" for liaison. The Aeronca O-58 became the L-3. For the war effort, the Aeronca Aircraft Company produced 1,798 L-3s, 253 TG-5 gliders, and in cooperation with the Fairchild Aircraft Company, Aeronca built 620 PT-19A military trainers known as the Cornell.

A factory-fresh Aeronca 0-58B waits out side of the factory for delivery in early 1942. The added military equipment increased the gross weight to 1850 pounds. The 0-58/L-3 series of liaison aircraft was in such demand that almost 50 of them were impressed into military service in the Spring of 1942 alone! (NASM)

An Aeronca 0-58B banks away showing the words U S Army painted on the bottom of the wings, along with the U S national insignia with the red disc in the center of the insignia. Low speed maneuverability in the Aeronca was outstanding. (NASM)

As to the use of the O-58/L-3, we know it was a very rugged trainer aircraft used in many flight schools. The L-3 found itself out on the west coast flying patrols looking for Japanese submarines. In 1942 and 1943, the Free French used the L-3 as a trainer and general liaison aircraft. The L-3 saw general duty in North Africa, in France after the Normandy invasion, and in the South Pacific. In United States military duties overseas, the units with L-3s were U.S. Army units. Army Air Corps liaison units did use the L-3 in com-

The flightline, showing six new Aeronca 0-58As, is near a dirt strip for flying operations. The 0-58 could fly out of almost anything that was level for a few hundred feet, due to the low pressure balloon tires utilized on them. The photograph is dated 1941, but the location is unknown. (Minnesota Air Guard Museum)

bat, also. An L-3 was shot down by the Japanese during the retaking of Manila in the Philippines. Also an L-3 was shot down while directing artillery fire in North Africa. The Army liaison L-3 was a flexible monoplane, and served in all theaters of operations. Short take-off and landing requirements, easy maintenance, and low speeds made them ideal for artillery spotting, troop movements, general liaison courier chores, and observation. Happily for the crew, they were very difficult to shoot down, and if hit, the L-3 had considerable gliding capabilities. Bullets easily passed through the canvas covering usually doing little damage. Also, as the enemy learned the hard way, if you shoot at an liaison aircraft, you could have a lot of artillery down on you very fast. Therefore, they were not shot at usually.

All L-3s were declared surplus after V-J day, and were widely purchased very economically by the civilian market—both in the United States and overseas. Many still exist today.

Aeronca L-3D, 43-2823, was powered by a Continental 65 HP engine. Since very few L-3s were sent overseas, this is a probably a staged photograph with a Waco UCG-4A in the background. Aircraft serial numbers were frequently added on when the aircraft was assigned to a unit. (NASM)

(Above) *Very few Aeronca L-3 were sent overseas, but these were. The photograph was taken on Christmas Island in the Pacific in 1944. Most of the aircraft have their tails painted white, for easy identification. (Army Aviation Museum)*

(Below) *An Aeronica L-3C is blessed by a priest in Mascara, Morocco in April of 1943 upon transfer to the Free French forces in North Africa. The rudder already has a French red/white/blue marking on it. The American insignia on the fuselage has a yellow surround on it. (M.J. Strok)*

AERONCA O-58/L-3 MODEL 65TC GRASSHOPPER

L-3-AE ex O-58

L-3A-AE ex O-58A

L-3B-AE ex O-58B

L-3C-AE Same as L-3B-AE but with a radio. Engine was the 65 HP O-170-3. Total of 490 were built. Serial numbers were 43-1471 through -1960. These were at first given the serial numbers 42-60281 through -60777, but were cancelled.

L-3D-AE Eleven impressed Model 65 TF Defender tandem two-seaters with 65 HP Franklin 4AC-176 engine.

L-3E-AE Twelve impressed Model 65TC Defender tandem two-seaters with 65 HP Continental A-65-8 engine.

L-3F-AE Nineteen impressed Model 65 CA Super Chief side-by-side two seaters with a 65 HP Continental A-65-8 engine.

L-3G-AE Four impressed Model 65C Chief side-by-side two seaters with a 65 HP O-145-B1 engine.

L-3H-AE One impressed Model 65TL Defender. Same as the L-3D-AE but with a 65 HP O-145-B1 engine.

L-3J-AE One impressed Model 65TC Defender. Same as L-3E-AE but with a 65 HP Continental A65-3 engine.

The **L-3D** through **L-3J** impressions were allocated serial numbers 43-2809 through -2858, but no precise allocations are known, although not all the serials were taken up. Also, an L-3F-AE impressment (serial number 4081 was NC33876) was serial number 42-78044.

YO-58 Four aircraft were serial numbered 42-456 through -459 with a 65 HP YO-170-3 engine.

O-58 Same as the YO-58 but with a 65 HP O-170-3 engine. 50 were built with the serial numbers 43-2809 through -2858.

O-58A Same as the O-58 but with a wider fuselage, enlarged windows for better observation, 20 were built with the serial numbers 42-7793 through -7812.

O-58B Same at the O-58A but with equipment changes. 335 were built with the serial numbers 42-14713 through -14797 and 42-36075 through -36324. Redesignated as the L-3B-AE and 540 more were built with the serial numbers 42-38458 through -38497 and 43-26754 though -27253. Some were loaned to the U.S. Navy as JR-1s. The quantity is unknown, but they flew out of Olay Naval Air Station in California.

XTG-5-AE Three seat training glider version of the L-3 with a redesigned forward fuselage and tandem seats, with the instructor in front. Four prototype conversions were cancelled with the serial numbers 42-68302 through -68305.

TG-5-AE 250 were built using the serial numbers 42-57229 through -57478. An additional three were diverted to the U.S. Navy with the serial numbers 43-12493 through -12495.

LNR Three TG-5-AE (42-57457, -57461, and -57462) were diverted to the U.S. Navy to become Bureau of Aeronautics 36422 through 36424.

AERONCA O-58/L-3 Grasshopper

Wing span—35 feet
Length—21 feet, 0 inches
Height—7 feet, 8 inches
Wing area—158 square feet
Empty weight—865 pounds
Gross weight—1,800 pounds
Engine—Continental 0-170-3 (A-65-8) with 65 HP
Crew—one or two
Maximum speed—87 MPH
Cruise speed—75 MPH
Climb—400 feet per minute
Ceiling—7,750 feet
Range—190 miles

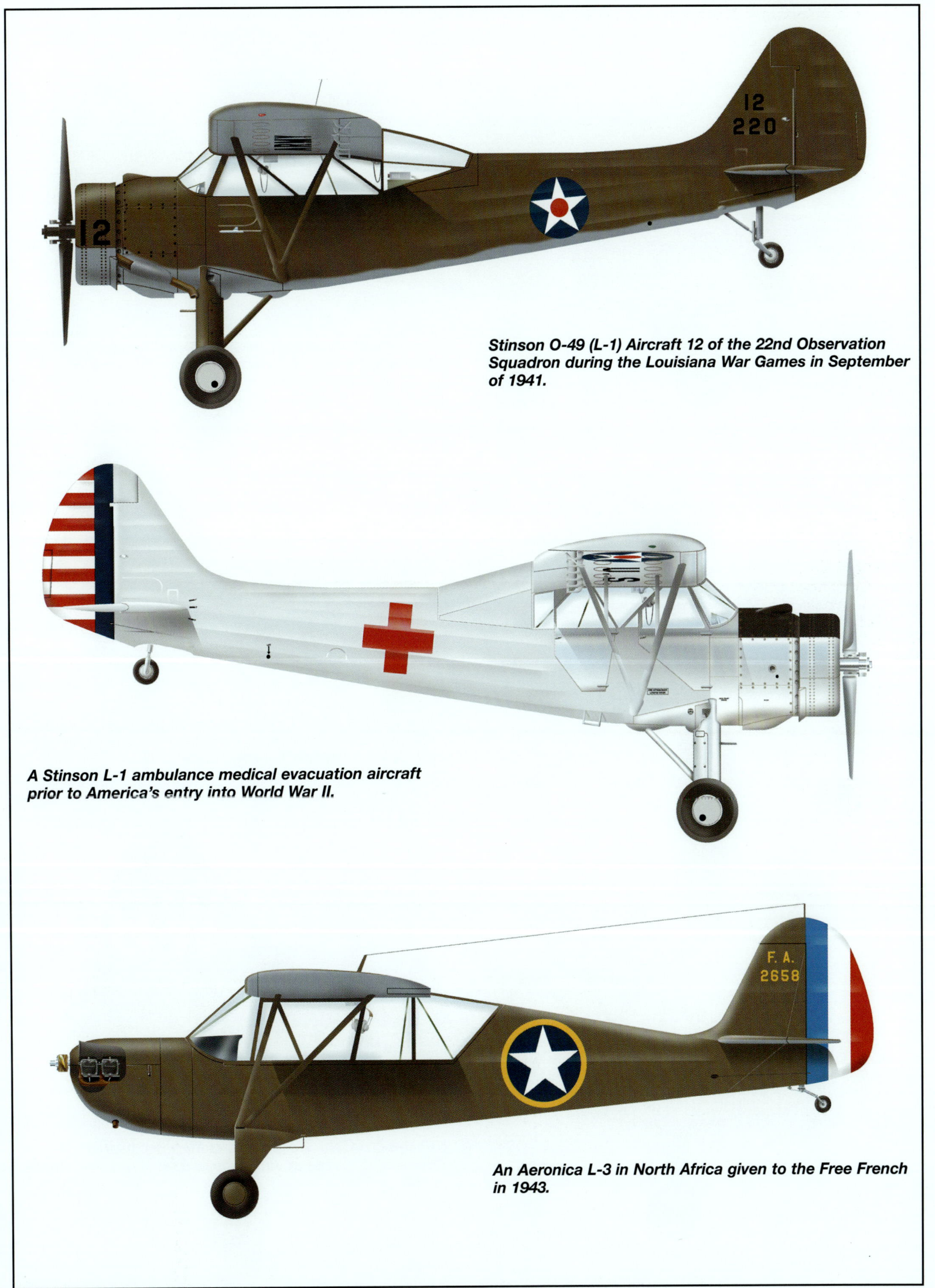

Stinson O-49 (L-1) Aircraft 12 of the 22nd Observation Squadron during the Louisiana War Games in September of 1941.

A Stinson L-1 ambulance medical evacuation aircraft prior to America's entry into World War II.

An Aeronica L-3 in North Africa given to the Free French in 1943.

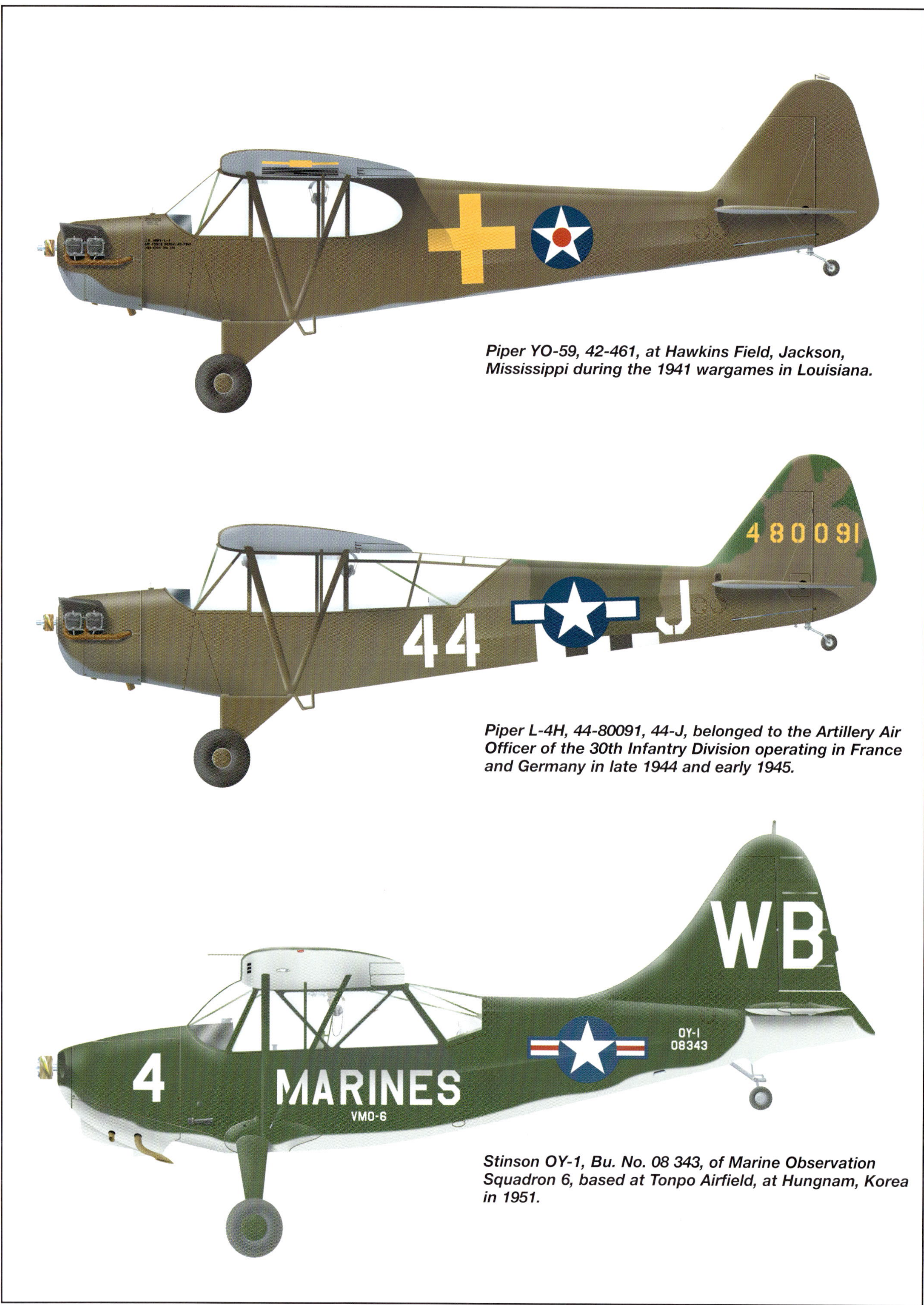

Piper YO-59, 42-461, at Hawkins Field, Jackson, Mississippi during the 1941 wargames in Louisiana.

Piper L-4H, 44-80091, 44-J, belonged to the Artillery Air Officer of the 30th Infantry Division operating in France and Germany in late 1944 and early 1945.

Stinson OY-1, Bu. No. 08 343, of Marine Observation Squadron 6, based at Tonpo Airfield, at Hungnam, Korea in 1951.

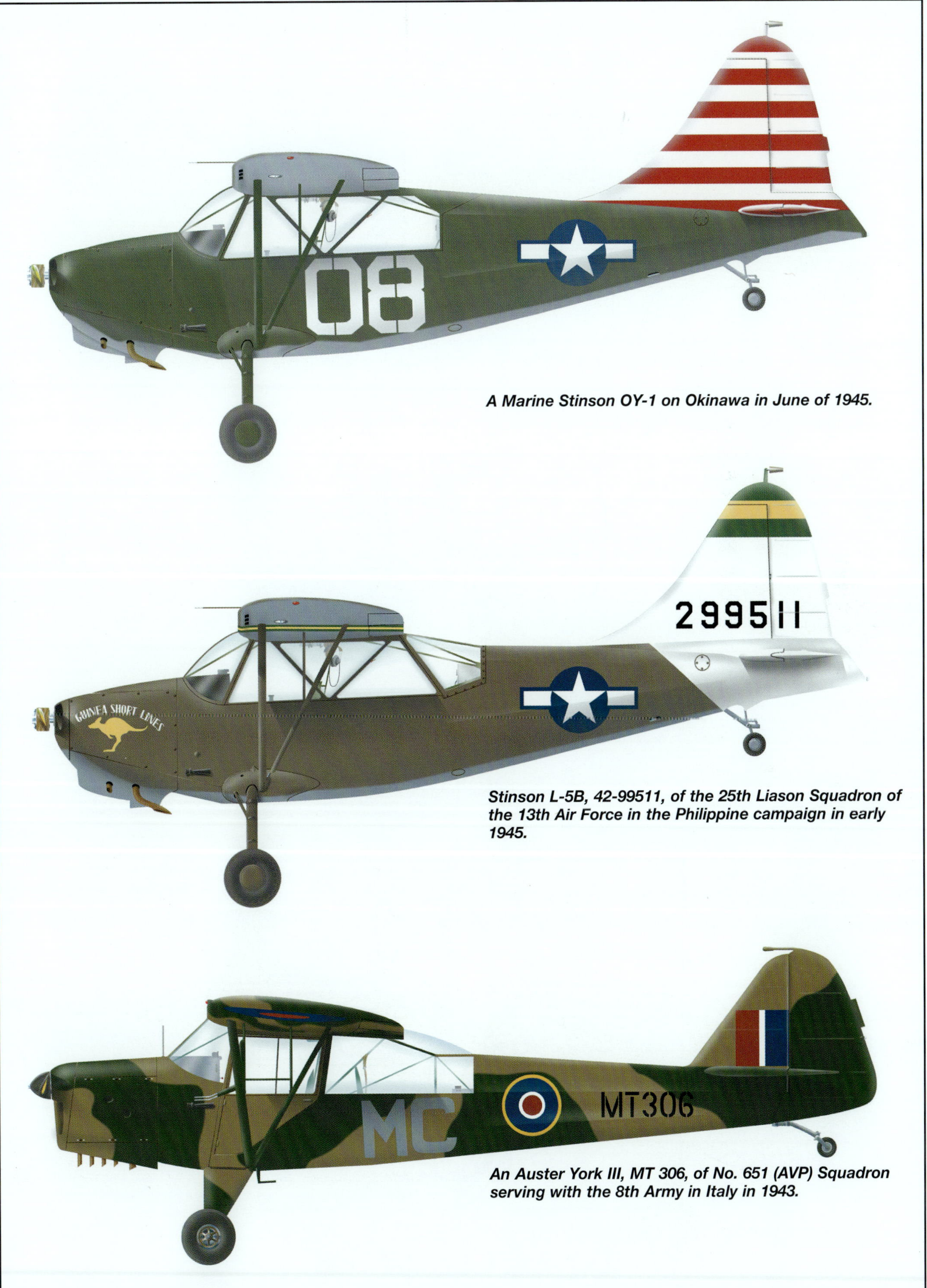

A Marine Stinson OY-1 on Okinawa in June of 1945.

Stinson L-5B, 42-99511, of the 25th Liason Squadron of the 13th Air Force in the Philippine campaign in early 1945.

An Auster York III, MT 306, of No. 651 (AVP) Squadron serving with the 8th Army in Italy in 1943.

An Taylorcraft LBT-1 (JG-6) of the U.S. Navy during "Atomic Bomb" glide tests in 1944.

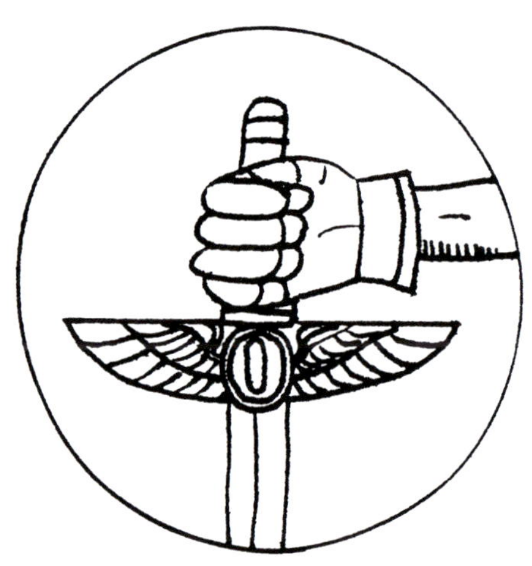

25th Liaison
Squadron

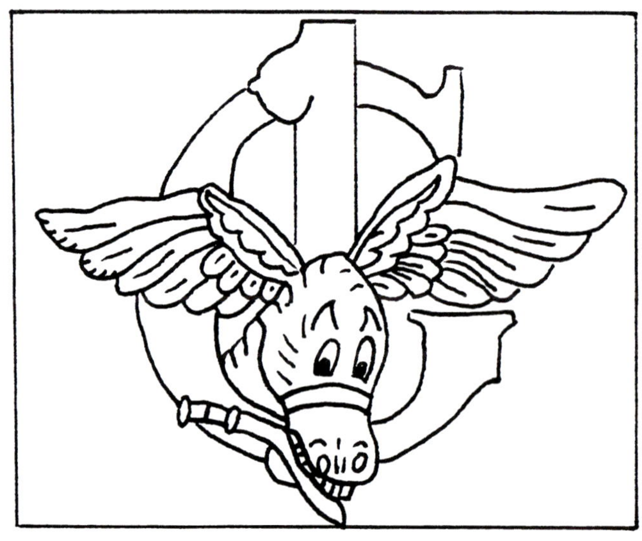

1st Air Commandos

CHAPTER FIVE

PIPER O-59 / L-4 Grasshopper

The Piper L-4 Cub or Grasshopper was designed by the man who originally designed the E-2 Taylor Cub. It was in 1930 that C. Gilbert Taylor and his brother organized the Taylor Aircraft Corporation at Bradford, Pennsylvania.

The company was reorganized in 1931 as the Depression took effect, but the company was renamed as the Taylorcraft Aircraft Corporation. The only real change was the addition of local oilman William T. Piper as secretary-treasurer of the new company.

The Piper Cub story now really begins when in 1935 in the middle of the Depression, when the President of the company, C. Gilbert Taylor, sold his share of the Taylorcraft Aircraft Corporation to William T. Piper. From 1931 until 1935, Piper had financed the very successful Taylor Cub. This was a single engine, tandem seat, monoplane which prospered because of its economy, low price and ease of maintenance. This was truly a creation of the world-wide economic depression. Various differences of opinion led to the parting of Taylor and Piper. Piper kept the company, the Cub and all of the manufacturing rights, and Taylor received money.

A SSGT stands by his Piper 0-59 on the sandy beach in Texas in late 1941 or early 1942. The Piper 0-59 belonged to the 111th Observation Squadron. The Piper could land just about anywhere there was a few hundred feet of level ground. It also had low pressure, balloon tires. (Tom Hale)

A freshly uncrated and assembled Piper L-4 in England awaits delivery to its unit in the summer of 1943. In the background are RAF Handley Page Halifax bombers. (Jim Mesko)

Piper 0-59A, serial number 42-36639, of the 111th Observation Squadron of the 68th Observation Group, flies along the Texas country-side in July of 1942. The unit added the serial number on the tail, and also the diagonal fuselage stripe. Color of the strip's center is white, but the other colors are unknown. (Tom Hale)

Three mechanics relax in front of "Pappy," a Piper L-4 that was a squadron hack of the 4th Fighter Group based at Debden, England. One of the markings of the 4th Fighter Group was red noses. This carries over to the squadron hack also. Even the prop tips and leading edges are painted red. In the background is an early camouflaged Boeing B-17G. (Mark Copeland)

Piper operated the business under the name of Taylor Aircraft Corporation for a short time, but this caused confusion, since Taylor started his own aircraft company. So the company was reorganized and renamed the Piper Aircraft Corporation in Lock Haven, Pennsylvania. At this point, Piper was the President, Treasurer, and general manager.

One of Piper's engineers was a man named Walter Jamouneau who fine-tuned the Cub design so as not to disrupt production very much. He changed the designation of the E-2 Cub into the J-3 Cub (J stood for Jamouneau, of course). The first model of the J-3 was produced in 1937, and this evolved into the YO-59 which became the L-4. All were basically the same aircraft.

In 1938, with the declaration of a need to train pilots, the J-3 was there to do the job, efficiently and effectively. The transition from J-3 to O-59 was completed by simply cutting away the fabric and putting on a transparent plexiglass panel in the "greenhouse" area.

During the Louisiana war games, the North American O-47, the Stinson O-49, and the Curtis O-52 competed with the Piper J-3, and they more than met their match, although the Stinson O-49 came close. There seemed to be nothing that the versatile J-3 could not do or accomplish at a fraction of the cost. With the Piper J-3 Cub redesignated the O-59, there was no end to the demands placed on the Cub! They did the job, and they did it well. With the throttle wide open to the stops, they would do less than 100 miles per hour.

The O-59 which became the L-4, was operated in greater numbers than any other liaison or observation type during the formative years of what would eventually become the modern Army's air arm of Army Aviation, and it played a significant role in shaping the operational doctrine that guided Army aviation activities until the early years of the Vietnam War. Examples of several L-4 variants did, in fact, remain in the Army's inventory into the early 1950s. The L-4 provided the basic airframe from which two other signifi-

This ex-Danish Piper Cub J-2 (OY-DUP) was seized by the German Luftwaffe from Denmark. It was coded GP+QP, werke number 1319. It was re-captured by American forces in France or Germany in late 1944 or early 1945. (James Crow)

The same re-captured Piper has "Don't Shoot! U.S.A." written on the nose, and the U S insignia painted on the wing. These photographs were taken shortly after its seizure, and before the Americans had time to paint over the Swastika on the tail. (James Crow)

cant Army aircraft were developed.

The ubiquitous Piper L-4 first entered Army service in 1941 during the Louisiana war games, as the O-59, when it was one of three commercial light plane types selected for evaluation in the artillery observation and general liaison roles. Like the other two aircraft chosen for testing, the Taylorcraft Model D (L-2), and the Aeronca Model 65TC Defender (L-3), the Piper J-3-65 Cub was a light, two-place, high-wing monoplane of simple metal and fabric construction. Speed was not an especially important factor in the evaluation, and the Cub's good short-field performance and ease of maintenance made it an ideal Army co-operation aircraft.

The 65 horsepower engine allowed the L-4 to operate on automobile gasoline. This fact proved vital to many liaison pilots. There were many times when the pilots would land their L-4s in a field, drain the gas from a truck or jeep or a tank or obtain a couple of 5 gallon jerrycans, and then pour it into their L-4s and be off to complete their assigned mission. The L-4 fuel tank only held 12 gallons of gas. That was enough for about three hours of flight time!

The Department of Air Training was formed on June 6, 1942 at the Army artillery school at Fort Sill, Oklahoma. Liaison aviation and Army Aviation was born on that date! Most of the airplanes used to train the pilots were Piper L-4s. The L-4 was produced in the greatest number of any of the liaison aircraft used during World War II. Look at these impressive production figures. A total of 5,424 Piper L-4s were manufactured and delivered to the military between February 3, 1942 and August 22, 1945. In addition, Piper built 14,125 civilian Cubs from 1938 until 1947. No civilian Cubs were built from February of 1942 through August of 1945.

This Piper L-4 was the squadron hack of the 362nd Fighter Squadron, 357th Fighter Group. The group's checkerboard markings carried over to the Piper, also. The name painted between the side door and the engine is "Balls Out." (Jim Crow)

Another squadron hack of the 4th Fighter Group based in Debden, England, was this Piper L-4 taking off from the grass infield at Debden. Of course, it had a red nose. A close look at the background shores a few parked P-51s, and two P-51s in the landing pattern. (Mark Copeland)

Like Aeronca and Taylorcraft, the Piper Aircraft Company was asked in 1942 to evolve a training glider from their basic liaison aircraft that they were building at that time. This was mainly accomplished by removing the engine and the landing gear and substituting a new front fuselage with an extra seat for the instructor. A new simple cross axle landing gear with individually actuated hydraulic brakes and a steerable tailwheel, completed the undercarriage. The vertical tail control surfaces area was increased and full controls were provided at each of the three seats. Three of these gliders were produced for the U.S. Navy and designated the XLNP-1. Two hundred and fifty were produced for the Army under the designation TG-8. The Navy also used many of the Piper L-4s for primary naval flight training and designated them as the

Piper L-4, 42-36413, was originally built as an 0-59A. The unit is unknown, but the D-Day stripes and the leather flying jacket that the pilot is wearing, means that the photograph was taken in late 1944 or early 1945 in France or Germany. This aircraft carries one of the largest nose art "teeth and eyes" ever seen on an L-4. (Jim Crow)

Piper L-4H, 43-30233, of the 79th Infantry Division, is backdrop for a couple of happy GIs. This photograph was taken in Germany in 1945, either just before or after the war ended. (Jim Crow)

NE-1. They were primarily to serve at Naval Air Station training bases. The Navy acquired 230 NE-1s which were basically similar to the U.S. Army L-4s with Continental O-170-3 engines. Twenty NE-2s were similar. The Navy also acquired, in 1942, 100 HE-1 ambulance versions of the Piper J-3C with Lycoming O-235-2 engines and capable of carrying one stretcher plus the pilot. These aircraft were redesignated AE-1 when the H designation was assigned to helicopters in 1943.

In early 1943, Capt. Theodore Petras, personal pilot for the commanding general of the 1st Marine Division, suggested to his boss, Major General A. A. Vandergrift, an idea to form a light plane squadron within the division to handle aerial reconnaissance and artillery spotting. Thus the Marine Observation Squadron (VMO) was born. General Vandergrift was enthusiastic about having an air liaison detachment to his division. After the Guadalcanal campaign was over, the division was deployed to Australia for rest and replenishment. Then the division was sent to Goodenough Island off the New Guinea coast to set, stage, and train for the next operation. While there, it was noticed that the U.S. Army had lots of L-4s. General Vandergrift talked to General MacArthur about obtaining some L-4s. His request was granted, and the division was delivered a dozen L-4s. The unit to operate the L-4s was designated the 1st Provisional Air Liaison Unit.

The unit lost little time in getting into the air. An L-4 was rigged with floats and utilized in that role for the Marines. The L-4s did much more than serve as taxies for the brass. The terrain was heavy jungle around Cape Gloucester and New Guinea, and the existing maps of the area were not very accurate. To solve the problem of target acquisition, the division artillery called on the Cubs. It worked very well! The beginning

Piper L-4s served in every theatre of the war. Here this Piper L-4 is in the Panama Canal Zone in 1943. Nose art was even allowed in the Panama Canal Zone as shown by these "teeth and eyes." The name of the aircraft was "Crying Tiger." This might have been one of many Pipers "impressed" in the Panama Canal Zone early in the war. (Jim Crow)

Ken Thoen was with the 357th Fighter Group, 9th Air Force in Neubiberg, Germany in the summer of 1945. The Piper L-4 has the code of the 362nd Fighter Squadron. The L-4 was painted overall silver—a rarity in those days in Europe. (Jim Crow)

of the VMO's brought an end to Piper L-4 operations six weeks before the invasion of Peleliu. VMO-3, a regularly assigned VMO with naval aviators and brand new OY (Stinson L-5) aircraft, maintained by Navy school-trained mechanics, joined the 1st Marine Division, and all of the other Marine divisions also at this time.

Back in the ETO, a German prisoner of war said that more fear was generated by the sight of a L-4 than any other allied aircraft. When they saw a L-4, they knew that artillery fire was sure to follow—masses of artillery fire. Therefore, L-4s and L-5s were rarely shot at, and, if they were shot at, artillery was only moments away from falling on the source of that fire. But, if a liaison aircraft, like the L-4, was hit, since it was covered by canvas, the bullets easily passed through. Basically, only if the engine or the pilot was hit, was the aircraft brought down.

The L-4 was the first airplane to fly off an aircraft carrier and land in North Africa during that campaign. The L-4 was the first airplane to fly off the top of a specially built deck above the top of an LST. The deck was 12 feet wide and 200 feet long. To launch the L-4, the LST had to swing around into the wind and open its diesel engine wide open—all of 8 knots! A Piper L-4 was the first allied aircraft to land in North Africa, a Piper L-4 was the first allied aircraft to land in Europe after D-Day, a Piper L-4 was the first allied aircraft to land in Paris after the liberation of that city, and a Piper L-4 was the first allied aircraft to land on Okinawa!

Of the three types of liaison aircraft used in the

General Dwight Eisenhower was a private pilot before the war started. He knew the value of the Liaison-type of aircraft. Ike is shown here in the backseat of one of his favorites—the Piper L-4! (NASM)

ETO, (L-1, L-4, and L-5), the Piper L-4 was the most numerous which was officially known as the "Grasshopper," but most GIs just called it the "Cub."

The first group of liaison aircraft to reach the ETO was on September 16, 1942. They were 36 new Piper L-4Bs (serial numbers 43-591 through 43-626). They were initially assigned to the Eighth Air Force, then being established in England, but they were actually intended for the Field Artillery. The first ten aircraft that were uncrated and assembled, were for the Field Artillery of the 1st Infantry Division at Tidworth, Wiltshire, but when that unit's departure to North Africa in late October for Operation Torch, the L-4s were diverted to the Artillery Section of II Corps, then also at Tidworth. They then set up an Air Observation Post School for L-4 pilots. By February of 1943, they were all gone to North Africa. By then, L-4s were also in service with the 29th Infantry Division—all four Field Artillery Battalions and Division Artillery Headquarters.

No military Piper L-4s were ever given to another foreign country. All military procured by the U S military went to the U S military. However, some foreign countries had some Cubs built for their military. Here, a Cub of the Brazilian Air Force is shown as Belem Do Para Pan Am air field in February of 1942. The first sergeant of the 1st Provisional Marine Company, U S Marine Corps, is standing under the wing. (Jim Crow)

Piper L-4H, 43-30215, belongs to the 2nd Infantry Division, and is being prepared for another mission, probably in late 1944 in Europe. (Jim Crow)

A second shipment of L-4Bs arrived in England on October 5, 1942, followed by three more shipments in November. From then until the end of the war, shipments of L-4s continued at frequent intervals for issue to the many U.S. Army units which arrived in England prior to D-Day.

The L-4 pilots were generally Field Artillery officers, but liaison sergeant pilots were also very common. Both officer and NCO pilots wore silver wings similar to those of the USAAF, but with the letter L super-imposed on them. Most were initially trained by the USAAF, often at civilian contract schools, but their advanced liaison training, including artillery fire direction and short field operations, were completed at the Air Training Department of the School of Field Artillery at Fort Sill, Oklahoma.

In addition to Field Artillery use, 32 of the first shipments of L-4s went to an Eighth Air Force unit, the 153rd Reconnaissance Squadron of the 67th Observation Group. Many other L-4s of subsequent shipments, were delivered to various AAF combat units and headquarters for use on courier duties. Eleven L-4s were assigned to VIII Bomber Command, and six L-4s were assigned to VIII Fighter Command for distribution to combat groups.

Of these L-4 assignments, as each unit passed through England or was stationed in England, all received Piper L-4s, 2,788 of which reached England. Of this total, 213 were L-4As, 370 were L-4Bs, and 1,327 were L-4Hs, and 870 were L-4Js.

They were assigned to 42 Infantry, 15 Armored, and 4 Airborne divisions of the U.S. Army, and also to 16 Corps Headquarters, 5 Field Artillery Brigades, 62 Field Artillery Groups, and 7 Army headquarters.

Many L-4s came to Europe by way of North Africa, and landings in Italy, and Southern France. After D-Day, other shipments were transported directly from America to France.

Early in 1945, a few L-4s that were assigned to AAF units in England, were painted overall aluminum or silver.

L-4s did not have the USAAF serial numbers painted on the tail from the factory. They were applied by AAF Base Depots, or other Air Service Commands, or the units themselves. Therefore, there are many variations in shape, size, and style of L-4 tail serial numbers. But many L-4s in Europe remained without tail serial numbers—particularly those L-4s assigned to the Fifth and Seventh Armies in Italy and Southern France. The entire interior of the L-4 was painted in Olive Drab.

The last recorded air-to-air kill in the European Theatre of Operations occurred in late April of 1945, when an U.S. Piper L-4 unarmed observation aircraft named "Miss Me", belonging to the Fifth Armored Division, spotted a German Fieseler Storch over Germany. The L-4 pilot Lt. Duane Francies and his observer, dived on the German aircraft and shot it down using only their personal .45 caliber automatic pistols. They landed and captured the German pilot and observer. It was the only World War II German plane shot down with a handgun!

The number of L-4s still flying today attest to the value and true stamina of this liaison aircraft. The loads that they carried were unbelievable! The L-4 worked equally well on floats and many served in Alaska and in the Aleutian Campaigns in the float configuration.

If the truth be known, the L-4 created more chaos and destruction among the enemy while rescuing more Allied wounded and hurried the end to enemy hostilities more than all the allied bombers and fighters put together! In fact, in the Italian campaign, Italian and

A V Corps Artillery Piper L-4 comes to grief in the winter of 1944/1945 in Europe. Piper L-4s operated very well "in the field" with the troops. (Jim Crow)

An enlisted man stands by the tail of a Piper L-4, in the markings of the 53rd Fighter Squadron of the 36th Fighter Group in Europe late in the war. A bare metal Republic P-47 Thunderbolt "Razorback" is in the background. (Jim Crow)

German soldiers were given a 15 day pass for every L-4 that they shot down and destroyed!

When the dust settled and the cheering died down after VE-day, the Army and Navy, as we all know, got rid of a lot of their over-sized inventory of flying heavy metal by sending them back home and then either selling them or scrapping them in a wholesale manner.

For all of the L-4s left scattered over Europe, it was another story. Too bulky and not high enough in priority to be sent back, these planes were sold off to local clubs, aviation schools, and civilians of American allies. Therefore, hundreds of these L-4s still exist.

Yet over the past 50 plus years, attrition has dwindled the number of L-4s considerably. How many are still flying in Europe is rather difficult to pin-point. Colin Smith of Sawbridgenorth, England guesses that there are more than 300 L-4s still registered with most of them still flying over the English countryside. But, wherever they are or whatever they are for, these planes are real warbirds, having seen combat in the European war zone.

Late in the war in Europe, the Brazilian Air Force deployed some squadrons of military aircraft contributing to the war effort on the part of the Allies. One of the squadrons was a liaison squadron of Piper L-4s. All of the L-4s were in Italy. Records show that 32 were transferred to the Brazilians, except for one plane. Ten L-4s were taken back to Brazil after the war. The exception seems to have gone direct from the USA to make a total of 11 planes to Brazil. Of those remaining in Europe at the end of the war, 4 became Italian Civil and one became Swiss civil registered. All of the remained returned to the USA and USAAF use. Those in Brazilian became L4-3057 and L4-3070 through L4-3079 in Brazilian Air Force use.

The Piper L-4 series of aircraft were the cheapest combat aircraft built for the American Armed forces during World War II. The unit price was approximately $2,000 per copy, depending upon which contract they were ordered under, and the quantity. This was perhaps the best "bang for the buck" aircraft during the entire war! Also, L-4s are probably the largest number of true war birds in existence!!

French pilots attached to the Zéme Division Blindée of General LeClerc. The group landed in Normandy in June, 1944, helped liberate Paris, then fought into Germany. Insignia under cockpit is that of France (John Zeltwanger via James Crow)

(Above) ***Lt. Ken Thorpe's Piper L-4 H, 43-29635, (59-Y of the 196th FA Bn.), is parked on the Avenue de la Grande Armée, near the Arc de Triomphe, shortly after the liberation of Paris on August 25, 1944 (G. Grod)***

(Below) ***The first Piper YO-59s were delivered to the U.S. Army in time to participate in some of the 1941 war games. This YO-59 is 42-461, which was delivered on September 17, 1941, and was photographed at Hawkins Field at Jackson, Mississippi. (Boardman C. Reed)***

PIPER O-59/L-4 CUB VERSION OF THE J-3C-65

L-4-PI ex O-59

L-4A-PI ex O-59A

L-4B-PI Same as the L-4A but without radio equipment. Engine was the 65 HP O-170-3. 980 were built with the serial numbers 43-491 through -1470. (Piper serial numbers 9676 to 10291.) This was contract number W535ac30116 signed in August of 1942. Value of contract was $2,796,645.31 including the aircraft and spare parts. They were completed by the end of October of 1942.

L-4C-PI Eight impressed Model J-3C-65s with 65 HP O-145-B1 engine. The first two were 42-79557 and -79557 (Piper serial numbers 6170 and 6167), were ex-Panama civilian aircraft registered R-22E and R-23E, were initially designated UC-83As. The other six were 43-2923, -2925, -2927, -2932, -2959, and -2967.

L-4D-PI Five impressed Model J-3F-65s with a 65 HP Franklin 4AC-176 engine. The serial numbers were 43-2914, -2924, -2992, -2995 and -2996.

L-4E-PI 17 impressed Model J-4Es with a 75HP Continental A-75-9 engine. Used for pre-glider training. One aircraft, 42-79555, Piper serial number 1323, was ex-Panama civil registration R-11E. It was initially designated UC-83B. Serial numbers were 43-2941, 2954 through -2958, -2973 through -2974, -2989 through -2990, and -3003 through -3008.

L-4F-PI 43 impressed Model J-5As with 75 HP Continental A75-9 engine. Four were impressed in Panama and originally designated as a UC-83. The four in Panama were serial numbered 42-79551 through -79554 with Piper serial numbers of 513, 514, 515, and 211 respectively. They were ex-Panama civil registry RX-25, RX-26, RX-95, and RX-27. The remainder of the impressions were serial numbers 42-57507 (Piper Number 1080, ex-NC3871), 42-107425 (Piper Number 5928, ex-NC38393), and 43-2909, -2911, -2912, -2915 through -2920, -2922, -2926, -2930, -2931, -2934, -2935, -2937 through -2939, -2947 through -2949, -2991, -2999 through -3002, and 44-52988.

L-4G-PI 34 impressed Model J-5Bs with a 100 HP GO-145-C2 engine. Serial numbers were 43-2910, -2913, -2921, -2928, -2929, -2933, -2936, -2940, -2942 through -2946, -2948, -2950, -2951, -2963, -2971, -2972, -2975 though -2977, -2979, -2981 through -2988, -2994, -2997 and -2998.

L-4H-PI Same as the L-4B-PI, but with improved radios and a fixed-pitch propeller. 1801 were built. The serial numbers were 43-29247 through -30547 (Piper serial numbers 10538 through 11838), and 44-79545 through -80044 (Piper serial numbers 11841 through 12340).

L-4J-PI Same as the L-4H-PI but with a controllable-pitch propeller. 1680 were built. The serial numbers were 44-80045 through -80844 (Piper serial numbers 12341 through 13140), 45-4401 through -5200 (Piper serial numbers 13141 through 13940), and 45-55175 through -55254 (Piper serial numbers 13941 through 14020). In 1945, serial numbers 45-55216 through -55223 were cancelled and replaced by 45-55255 through -55257, -55259, -55263, -55264, and -55267. Also another 270 were ordered with the serial numbers 45-55255 through -55524, but were all cancelled as the end of the war approached.

UC-83-PI These were impressed in Panama. They were Model J-5As with a 75 HP O-170-1 engine. They were serial numbered 42-79551 (Piper serial number 513) ex-RX-25, 42-79552 (Piper serial number 515) ex-RX-26, 42-79553 (Piper serial number 514) ex-R95, and 42-79554 (Piper serial number 211) ex-RX-27. These were all redesignated as L-4F-PI in 1943.

UC-83A-PI These were Model J3L-65s with a 65 HP O-145 engine. They were impressed in Panama. They were serial numbered 42-79557 (Piper serial number 6170) ex R-22E, and 42-79558 (Piper serial number 6167) ex R-23E. They were redesignated L-4Cs in 1943.

UC-83B-PI This was a Model J-4A. It was also impressed in Panama. Its serial number was 42-79555 (Piper serial number 1323) ex R-11E.

YO-59 Four aircraft for evaluation. They were serial numbered 42-460 through -463. The engine was the O-170-3 with 65 HP.

O-59 The initial production model of which 140 were built. Serial numbers were 42-7813 through -7952.

O-59A Same as the O-59, but with enlarged cabin windows.948 were built. The serial numbers were 42-15159 through -15329 (Piper serial numbers 8278 through 8448), 42-36325 through -36824 (Piper serial numbers 8449 through 8948), 42-38380 through -38457 (Piper serial numbers 8949 through 9020), and 43-29040 through -29240 (Piper serial numbers 10339 through 10537).

TG-8-PI Three-seat training glider. 250 production models were built. The serial numbers were 43-3009 through -3258 (Piper serial numbers G1 through G250). An additional 3 were ordered for the US Navy as the LNP-1 with the serial numbers 43-12499 through -12501. Serial numbers 43-3065, -3070, and -3075 became XLNP-1s using Bureau of Aeronautics numbers 36425 through 36427.

HE-1 Ambulance version of the Model J-5C with hinged fuselage top decking for access to a stretcher and an O-235-2 engine. 100 were built for the US Navy. They were BuAero numbers 30197 through 30296. It was redesignated at the AE-1 in 1942.

NE-1 Same as the L-4B-PI but for the US Navy. It had a 65 HP O-170-2 engine. It had dual controls and tandem seats. 230 were built. BuAero numbers 26196 through 26425.

NE-2 Same as the NE-1 but with different radios. 20 were built. BuAero 29669 through 29688. Another 10 were cancelled with BuAero numbers 29689 through 29699.

XLNP-1 Three TG-8-Ps (43-3065, -3070, and -3075) were diverted to the US Navy as BuAero 36425 through 36427.

PIPER O-59/L-4 Grasshopper

Wing span—35 feet, 2 inches
Length—22 feet, 3 inches
Height—6 feet, 8 inches
Wing area—179 square feet
Empty weight—695 pounds
Gross weight—1,220 pounds
Engine—Continental 0-170-3 (A-65-8) with 65 HP
Crew—one or two
Maximum speed—85 MPH
Cruise speed—75 MPH
Climb—333 feet per minute
Range—190 miles
Stalling speed—39 MPH
Ceiling—9,300 feet

CHAPTER SIX

Stinson YO-54 / O-54 / O-62 / L-5 / OY

The Army liked the O-49 Vigilant, but they were also more interested in a low-cost fliver-type utility aircraft. The Vigilant was the Stinson Model 74, and the next was the Model 75. Work on the Model 75 was done at the Nashville facility. The prototype was a civilian registered airplane. It was tested with a new six-cylinder 125 HP Franklin engine, in which form the airplane received the Model 75C designation. Basic parts came from the civilian Model 10 Voyager. The Model 10 Voyager became the YO-54, but with large production orders for the O-49 Vigilant, Stinson built only six Voyagers for the U.S. Army in 1940. However, the French Air Force saw the Model 10 Voyager, liked it, and ordered 600 of them, Only a very small number of the Model 10 Voyagers/O-54s were delivered to France before the Germans occupied France. One Model 10 Voyager provided "air cover" during the Dunkirk evacuation, however, it was on its delivery trip to France, and then flew to England. In order to keep the new Model 10As from being taken over by the invading Germans, they were flown to England. All of them made it. It is unknown what happened to them, but there were very few of them that were in Europe at the time. The ones that did make it to England probably became squadron hacks, and/or courier aircraft.

The Model 75 program was then transferred to Wayne, Michigan to make way for the production of the O-49 Vigilant, and Vultee dive bombers. One of the main reasons that Vultee bought Stinson Aircraft at this time was to obtain the production facilities for Vultee's own aircraft.

Development of the military version continued as the Model 76, which flew for the first time on June 28, 1941. The aircraft had a 175 HP O-435-1 engine, and

The Stinson L-5 was a great aero-medical evacuation aircraft. Only one liter fit in the L-5, but it could operate out of short, very rough small landing fields. This evacuation took place in Luzon, the Philippines in early 1945. (Army Aviation Museum)

The L-5 could carry a litter patient for medical evacuation readily. L-5s saved many a wounded soldier or Marine, later to be replaced by helicopters in Korea and Vietnam. (William E. Davis)

The patient had lots of room in the L-5, versus some other aircraft, and he had windows on three sides of him. Here a minimally ill man is being loaded into a L-5 at or near Cox's Bazaar on the India-Burma border in early 1945. (Jim Crow)

Under the wing of Stinson L-5, 42-14891, are two rocket launching tubes for some "teeth." However, they were tested, but not authorized. But, "in the field," there were several adoptions of armed L-5s including Bazookas, light machine guns, etc. In the background is a Curtis P-40 in this October 10, 1944 photograph. (NASM)

fixed, full-span leading-edge slots. The production of the Model 76, better known to millions as the L-5 Sentinel. The L-5 was known as the "flying jeep." Its excellent short-field capabilities made it, by far, the most widely used Allied utility plane of World War II. It had a two-seat tandem cockpit, a slightly larger fuselage, higher operating weights due to military equipment, and military standard instruments and communications equipment.

The flying "Jeep" (don't ever call it a Cub or a Grasshopper to an L-5 driver's face or you will probably wonder what hit you) had very pleasant slow flying characteristics.

The L-5 was originally designated the O-62. The L-5 Sentinel was initially operated by the Army Air Forces, and did not reach the Army Ground Forces (Army Aviation) until 1943. The type quickly proved itself to be an excellent liaison and observation platform. The first Stinson L-5s reached England in 1944.

It became to second most widely used example of liaison aircraft, behind the Piper L-4 Cub.

With the allocation of AAF Liaison Squadrons to the ETO in early 1944, the Stinson L-5 Sentinels began to arrive in numbers. Some of the first L-5s to arrive in England were assigned to the 8th Weather Reconnaissance Squadron based at Watton, but most were assigned to the Ninth Air Force's Liaison Squadrons as they arrived. As a matter of fact, the first of these liaison squadrons to receive the L-5 was the

The L-5 served in all theatres of operations during the war. Here, numerous L-5s are parked at an airfield at Eschweg, Germany in April of 1945. Also parked around the airfield are a few P-51 Mustangs. (Minnesota Air Guard Museum)

A right echelon formation of six Stinson OY- 1s of VMO-3 over a Pacific island in 1945. The location is probably Okinawa. Very seldom did OY-1s operate other than alone. This is a posed photograph most likely after the end of hostilities. (David Manley collection)

"Miss Florida" was a L-5 that was stationed at Middle Wallop, England in May of 1944. The unit is unknown, and the aircraft look fairly clean and probably newly arrived in the ETO. (Minnesota Air Guard Museum)

Stinson L-5 named "Rome Express" was General Mark Clark's personal aircraft. The photograph was taken in Italy in 1944. 42-99033 was a standard L-5. (Jim Crow)

153rd Liaison Squadron, which evolved from the 67th Observation Group, which had been in England since late 1942. They were initially equipped with Douglas A-20s, Spitfires, and Piper L-4s, the 153rd was completely reorganized for its new role, and in the process, they exchanged the A-20s, and Spitfires, for more L-4s. Therefore, the squadron operated Piper L-4s and Stinson L-5s together. Most of the officer pilots and crews also departed with their aircraft, and in their place came AAF sergeant liaison pilots.

Similar liaison duties were performed by the L-5s of the 14th and 47th Liaison Squadrons, which arrived in England in April of 1944. The 47th was attached to the Third U.S. Army Headquarters at Knutsford in Cheshire, and the 47th was attached to the 12th Army Group headquarters in London. The next two liaison squadrons to arrive in England were the 125th and the 112th Liaison Squadrons that were intended to serve the Ninth U.S. Army and the Supreme Headquarters Allied Expeditionary Force (SHAEF), but they arrived in early June of 1944. Then more liaison squadrons arrived. The last unit to come to England was the 158th Liaison Squadron which arrived in December of 1944. It was attached to the 15th U.S. Army.

Thereafter, all new liaison squadrons went directly

Stinson L-5s were used as squadron hacks as some other L-Birds were also. This L-5 was one of the squadron hacks of the 86th Fighter Group of the 12th Air Force. This photograph was taken in Pisa, Italy in late 1944 or early 1945. The camouflage on the airplane was olive drab over neutral gray. (Jim Crow)

to France from America. The exact number of L-5s shipped to the ETO is not known, but with 32 aircraft assigned to each liaison squadrons, it is probable that the numbers was more than 400.

Despite its earlier insistence on just the L-4 for Army Ground Forces in the ETO, the AGF did obtain some L-5s from the Ninth Air Force prior to D-Day with the intention of allocating at least one L-5 to each Division, and Corps Artillery Headquarters for special

This L-5, 42-99464, is being inspected by a few "locals" in the Pacific or China theatre of operations. The actual location is unknown, but the date is 1944. (Jim Crow)

This L-5, 42-98106, was based in China, however it did not belong to the Ist Air Commando Group, but the unit is unknown. In the background is a Consolidated B-24. Consolidated owned Vultee Aircraft who owned Stinson Aircraft. They changed their name later to Convair - Consolidated Vultee Aircraft. (Jim Crow)

This L-5 had an all-white tail as a unit marking. The item under the fuselage attached to the aircraft appears to be a fuel slipper-tank of some sort. The photograph was taken some where in the Pacific theatre, probably in 1945. (Jim Crow)

duties. These included photographic and rapid visual reconnaissance, night observation missions, and courier flights in addition to those already undertaken by the liaison squadrons. While the L-4 reigned supreme as the artillery spotter aircraft, the cross-country limitations imposed by its short endurance and 75 MPH cruising speed rendered it less capable for the courier flights on which it was also frequently utilized.

Following D-Day, there was a mass exodus of liaison aircraft and squadrons from England to the Continent of Europe. Most of the L-5s were flown across the English Channel to France.

Because of its size and horsepower, it was not a true "Grasshopper." It was the only liaison airplane used by all branches of the U.S. military in all theatres of the

A L-5 cruises over the jungle at a fairly low altitude. In warmer climates, the pilot usually flew with the windows down for cooling, as shown in the photograph. The passengers rear door is missing, possible for better viewing or for air dropping small items or supplies. The unit is unknown, but it was in the Pacific or Asia somewhere. (Jim Crow)

The flightline, possibly on Okinawa, shows quite a few L-5s awaiting their next mission. (Jim Crow)

war and by most Allied forces during World War II. They were also used in the Korean Conflict a few years after the end of World War II, to serve in the roles they had proven so well in World War II. It was used from 1950 until 1952 by the U.S. military, and then given to a few more allies for operations for a few more years after that. It was replaced by the Cessna L-19/O-1 Birddog. The last L-5 on active duty was redesignated as the U-19B in 1962. It was used as a glider tow craft until as late as 1962 at the U.S. Air Force Academy in Colorado Springs, Colorado. A total of 4,481 were manufactured which is second only to the Piper L-4 whose production was 5,424. The U.S. Navy and U.S. Marine Corps had 306 L-5s that were called OY-1s. The RAF received 100 L-5s for use in Burma.

There were many which remained on active duty with the USAF and Marines until the mid-1950s, almost exclusively in the Continental United States. After the war, every National Guard unit had at least one L-5. They were scattered throughout other countries all over the world, too. Several thousand were sold as war surplus in 1945. The tough rugged air-

L-5, 42-98780, was camouflaged with olive drab over neutral gray, with a white star on the hub caps of the wheels. The nose art was a red arrow with "Lil Les" in the middle of the arrow, and a nude girl below the name in the arrow. The photograph was taken in the MTO in 1943 or 1944. (Jim Crow)

After the war was over in Europe, some men and equipment remained in Germany to keep the peace. This L-5 was 42-98562, and belonged to the 305th Bomb Group as a group hack. It was stationed at Lechteld, Germany in early 1946. In the background are some AT-6s. (Jim Crow)

This L-5 was one of the group hacks of the 86th Bomb Group of the 12th Air Force. The photograph was taken at Pisa, Italy in 1944. One of the colors of the stripes on the tail is white. The other color is unknown. (Jim Crow)

frame made the L-5 an excellent bush-country airplane for Alaska, Canada, Australia, New Zealand, Mexico, and India. Therefore, hundreds still exist world-wide today.

The U.S. Navy and U.S. Marine Corps operated 306 Stinson L-5s that were called OY-1s. All were transferred from the U.S. Army Air Forces, and they all had Bureau of Aeronautics numbers. The Navy liked them, and ordered 26 more, but this order was later cancelled. 29 of the OY-1s were fitted with modified equipment to become the OY-2. An additional 152 L-5s were transferred to the U.S. Navy, but retained their original U.S. Army serial numbers.

A U S Army L-5 was the victim of a Japanese artillery shell in Burma. The L-5 was written off. Nobody was hurt. This L-5 clearly shows how close to the front lines that some L-5 units operated. (Army Aviation Museum)

Lt. Dave Condon and his Stinson L-5, 42-98593, were the first allied aircraft to land on European soil after D-Day. Lt. Condon landed at Utah Beach on D-Day plus one, June 7, 1944, with black and white invasion stripes on the wings and tail. (Forty Years of Army Aviation by Richard K Tierny)

In 1943, when the Navy and Marines acquisition of the type began, Vultee merged with Consolidated, a few years earlier. Consolidated later became Consolidated Vultee Aircraft or shortened to Convair. Therefore, Consolidated Aircraft's Navy letter Y is in the designation of the OY-1.

Finally 40 Stinson L-5s were transferred to the RAF as Sentinel Is for use in the China-Burma-India theatre of operations. Also 60 L-5Bs were transferred to the RAF in the same theatre as Sentinel IIs. All 100 were delivered under lend-lease programs. The decision to supply the L-5 to the RAF was made by President Franklin D. Roosevelt at the Quebec Conference in November of 1943 with British Prime Minister Winston Churchill. RAF units that used the Sentinels were the Headquarters Squadrons and Flights of the 3rd Tactical Air Force, No. 221, No. 224,

A typical pilot is ready to go on the next liaison mission in the ETO in his L-5. The cockpit was very spacious, and visibility was tremendous. The windows were usually flown open when weather and climate allowed it. (Army Aviation Museum)

In combat zones, most U S military aircraft carried some form of nose art. Most tended towards nudes or double meaning sayings. The nose art on this L-5 displayed a beautiful nude on a cloud. Usually a name was associated with the nose art, but not in this case. (Tom Hale)

A Stinson L-5 Sentinel, during a visual reconnaissance sortie over the Philippines, has an observer in back that appears to have spotted something on the jungle-covered hills. (via Rene J. Francillio, Ph.D.)

and No. 225 Groups, and No. 194, No. 27, and No. 357 Squadrons. No. 357 Squadron was the "Special Duties Squadron" operating various aircraft on clandestine missions and operations.

In early 1945, an overall aluminum or silver finish was adopted on some L-5s that were assigned to AAF units This painting was done locally and probably just to L-5s that were still in England—not on the Continent of Europe. Therefore, there were very few L-5s ever painted in that color during the war. The interior of the L-5 was painted a zinc-chromate green.

The Army Ground Forces (AGF), usually Field Artillery, L-5s carried no unit or individual aircraft identification markings. However, prior to D-Day, two digit codes were adopted by Army Headquarters, Field Artillery Brigades, Field Artillery Groups, and all divisions. These numbers were painted in white ahead of the fuselage national insignia, and were followed by an individual aircraft identification letter.

Most Field Artillery (AGF), and Liaison Squadrons aircraft were "named," but it appears that "nose art," which was such a colorful feature of USAAF aircraft, did not meet the approval of the powers-that-be in the Army Ground Forces. So therefore, there was some "nose art" on liaison aircraft of the AGF, but it was fairly rare to see it.

Most USAAF squadrons "hacks" did feature nose art, especially with the Eighth and Ninth Air Forces. The standard two-character USAAF squadron codes

A flightline full of L-5s awaits the next liaison missions that they will be assigned to. Thc unit and date is unknown, as is the location, but it is probably taken in the Pacific or Asian theatre of operations. (NASM)

This Stinson L-5 of the 3rd Infantry Division, Division Artillery Headquarters, is carrying a lieutenant in the aft seat in the summer of 1944 in Prance. (Alfred W. "Dutch" Shultz)

were allocated to USAAF liaison squadrons.

The L-5 was a good rugged airplane, that was built to take a lot of punishment. It landed in cow pastures, wheat fields, in swamps, on railroads, on sandy beaches, and when mounted on floats, and many were on rough and smooth water, and also landings and takeoffs with the "Brodie System" installed. On a very rare occasion, it landed on a nice smooth runway.

U S Marine Lt. Stein of VMO-3 poses beside his Stinson OY-1 on Okinawa in mid-1945. Note the "Mae West" life preserver worn for over-water operations. (David Manley collection)

With the exception of the atomic bomb-carrying Boeing B-29 Superfortress, the liaison aircraft, in general, and the L-4 and L-5 in specific, could bring greater destructive power to bear on a selected target than any other aircraft in World War II, even though they were "David and Goliath" in size. (Boeing)

(Above) *Three Stinson OY-1s of VMO-3 in formation over a Pacific island in 1945. It was probably in the Ryukyu chain of islands of which Okinawa is the largest. The only unit markings are a white number on the tail. (David Manley collection)*

(Below) *U S Marine T/SGT Charles V. Cockran with MAG-31 prepares for another mission during the VMO-3 operations in 1945. The location is on the beach below Saastad Field on Motobu Peninsula on Okinawa. The only nose-art on this Stinson OY-1 is "T. S." (David Manley collection)*

(Below) *After the war, thousands of liaison aircraft were declared surplus. Thousands were bought at extremely low prices (sometimes the aviation gas in the full tanks, was worth more than what was paid for the aircraft). These surplus aircraft were used for a wide variety of purposes. Here, an L-5 has been converted into a crop duster, with a larger radial engine for power. Notice that this L-5 was made into a bi-plane for additional lift at heavy weights and low speed. (AAHS)*

STINSON O-54/L-5 SENTINEL

L-5-VW Same as the O-62-ST. An additional 1731 were built. The serial numbers were 42-14798 through -15072, and 42-98036 through -99573 with the 185 HP O-435-1 and a 12-volt electrical system.

L-5A-VW Same as the L-5-VW but with a 24-volt electrical system. A total of 688 were converted from L-5-VWs.

L-5B-VW This version had a deeper fuselage with a side loading hatch, internal provisions for a stretcher or 200 pounds of cargo. 730 were built. Serial numbers were 42-99574 through 99753, and 44-16703 through -17252.

L-5C-VW Same as the L-5B but with a K-20 camera in the fuselage. 200 were built. The serial numbers were 44-17253 through -17452.

L-5D-VW Project cancelled. Nothing built or developed.

L-5E-VW Same as the L-5C-VW, but with drooping ailerons operated in conjunction with the flaps for better STOL performance. 750 were built. The serial numbers were 44-17453 through -18202.

XL-5F-VW One converted L-5B (44-17103) was re-engined with a 185 HP O-435-2 engine.

L-5G-VW Same as the L-5E, but with a 190 HP O-435-11 engine. 115 were built. The serial numbers were 45-34911 through -35025.

YO-54 Six Stinson 10 Voyagers were acquired for evaluation. The serial numbers were 41-143 through -148. They were powered by the 80 HP O-170-1 engine. 600 were ordered by France, but none were delivered before Germany invaded.

O-62 Stinson Model V-76 version of the Voyager with an enlarged fuselage, and 185 HP O-435-1 engine. 275 were built. The serial numbers were 42-14798 through 015072.

L-9A-ST Eight impressed Model 10 Voyagers powered by 90 HP O-200-1 engine. Serial numbers were 42-88666 through -88673. They were previously designated AT-19As.

L-9B-ST Twelve impressed Model 10A Voyagers powered by a 90 HP Franklin 4AC-199-E3 engine. They were serial numbered 42-94130 (c/n 8254, ex-NC39454), 42-94136 (c/n 7804, ex-NC31559), 42-97051 (c/n 8256, ex-NC39456), 42-97430 (c/n 7919, ex-NC32271), 42-97432 (c/n 7787, ex-NC31538), 42-97434 (c/n 7780, ex-NC31530), 42-107278 (c/n 7797, ex-NC31540), 42-107406 (c/n 7845, ex-NC31596), 42-107407 (c/n 7906, ex-NC32258), 42-107408 (c/n 7764, ex-NC31514), 42-107409 (c/n 8002, ex-NC34602), and 42-107410 (c/n 7830, ex-NC31589).

OY The US Marine Corps version. A total of 306 were transferred from the US Army. They were BuA 02747 through 02756 (ex 42-99512 through -99521), 02751 through 02766 (ex 42-99690 through -99699), 02767 through 02776 (ex 44-16857 through -16866), 02777 through 02788 (ex 44-16957 through -16960), 03862 through 04008 (L-4E range), 04009 (ex 44-18137), 04010 through 04020 (L-4E range), 60460 through 60475 (ex 42-98448 through -98463), 60476 through 60491 (ex42-98528 through -98543), 60492 through 60507 (ex 42-98737 through -98752), 75159 through 75170 (ex42-98948 through -98959), 75171 through 75182 (ex 42-99040 through -99051), 120442 through 120446 (initially ordered at 04021 through 04025) (L-4E range), and 120447 through 120474 (L-4E range).

(**L-5-VW**) Forty were transferred to the RAF as Sentinel Is with the serial numbers KJ368 through KJ407. An additional 152 L-5s were transferred to the US Navy, retaining their original USAAF serial numbers. 26 OY-1s were cancelled. They were BuA 02789 through 02790, and 121415 through 121438. 29 OYs were fitted with modified equipment to become OY-2s.

(**L-5B-VW**) 60 were transferred to the RAF as Sentinel IIs with the serial numbers KJ408 through KJ467.

STINSON O-54/L-5

Wing Span—34 feet, 0 inches
Length—24 feet, 1 inch
Height—7 feet, 11 inches
Wing area—155 square feet
Empty weight—1,550 pounds
Gross weight—2,200 pounds
Engine—Lycoming 0-435-1 at 185 HP
Crew—one or two
Maximum speed—130 MPH
Cruise speed—115 MPH
Range—420 miles
Stalling speed—43 MPH
Ceiling—15,800 feet
Rate of climb—875 feet per minute

CHAPTER SEVEN

Interstate O-63 / L-6

The Interstate Engineering Corporation was a parts jobber building WW II bomb shackles, hydraulic units and the like for airplanes, in the former Moreland plant in El Segundo, California. They bought the plant for their expansion and there was still room enough to build airplanes. That was in 1938.

Deciding that a primary trainer for the CPTP (Civilian Pilot Training Program) was the most logical way to go for a small outfit like Interstate, President of Interstate was Don Smith. He hired Ted Woolsey to design and engineer a basic airframe. It became a school project because most of the detail work was handled by students of the Wiggins Trade School.

Various power plants were considered. Continental Motors was building a 50 HP, 65 HP, 75 HP and 85 HP engine. Lycoming was building a small 65 HP engine and a "geared" 90 HP engine. It was very doubtful as to which or how many engines would be available as Piper had contracted for the bulk of Continental's small engine production.

Interstate decided to certify its plane for all engines, 50 HP through 90 HP. It was found that the 50 HP engine would hardly get the airplane airborne with

A close up of the left aft portion of the cockpit windows of the L-6 shows the massive structure for support of the aircraft. It has more beams and angles in the superstructure than a massive bridge. (CSCM)

The prototype Interstate XL-6 shows U.S. Army Air Corps standard camouflage of olive drab over neutral grey with the red dot in the center of the U.S. insignia. The XL-6, serial 42-15895, was originally designated the XO-63. (NASM via Jim Johns)

just one person onboard. So, the 50 HP was scrapped in favor of the 65 HP through 90 HP engines. Most CPTP models used the 65 HP because parts were more readily available and this engine was more economical than the other engines. This airplane was a very late comer to the aircraft industry. Known as the Interstate Model S1A1 "Cadet" Approved Type Certificate (ATC) #737. It never achieved the dominance in the pre-war light plane industry as did the Piper, Aeronca, or Taylorcraft, but very soon became known as a nice airplane for flying.

When the United States became involved in World War II, contracts went out to produce more and more airplanes, especially trainers. Airplanes for every purpose were needed, so Interstate secured a contract to build a Liaison airplane for the Army. Their Interstate "Cadet" was re-designed was a counter-balanced rudder, flaps, expanded cockpit with greenhouse slanted outward so the pilot and observer could see directly below as well as directly above them. The engine chosen was the Franklin O-200-5 four cylinder horizontally opposed air cooled engine of 90 HP. This proved to be the fault of the airplane.

The Defense Department contracted for 250 of these aircraft to be designated as Interstate's Model L-6. They were assigned Army serial numbers 42-15895 (the prototype), and 43-2599 through 43-2808. Production of the L-6 went at an accelerated pace, but soon problems began to crop up. The engine had a severe overheating problem. New cowling and baffling was designed with no improvements. Also, a large oil cooler was added which helped somewhat, but it did not totally solve the problem. Most pilot training schools were located in the south and that area's warm weather seemed only to add to the problems.

There were not so many men trained in the L-6 as there should have been. This was a well constructed aircraft with forgiving qualities for the novice. The cockpit was not as small as the Taylorcraft L-2, Aeronca L-3, or the Piper L-4. And it could be flown from either the front or back seats.

When the war ended, the remaining Interstate L-6s were immediately declared surplus by the War Surplus Board. Many were bought for a very low price. Some were simply junked and some were used as spare parts. Interstate Aircraft Company was sold to Callaire merely for the metal and supplies that were on hand. Many of the surplus L-6s were put into civilian configuration and a Continental C-85-12 engine was used to replace the over-heating Franklin engine.

Like the L-2, the L-6 was never used in combat, and never went overseas. The L-6 was a little faster in flight, but could land and take-off in a very short distance just like the L-3 and the L-4. Had the L-6 been used in a war zone in combat, there is no doubt that it would have proven itself as a great performing liaison aircraft. The L-6 was 23 feet, 5 inches in length, 7 feet, 4 inches in height, and a 35 feet, 6 inches in wing-span. The empty weight was 1225 pounds, with a useful load of 550 pounds. The fuel capacity was 20 gallons with a maximum speed of 114 MPH and a cruise speed of 105 MPH. Landing speed with flaps was 48 MPH.

There were no cowling flaps on the Interstate L-6, but the cowling was larger than the fuselage for cooling as shown here. Also, it can be seen that the angle of the side windows was outward at the top. (SCM)

A closeup of the overhead windows of an L-6 from the rear, show massive plexiglass areas. One can just imagine what it was like operating the L-6 in the deserts of the southwest United States. (SCM)

CHAPTER EIGHT

Other Liaison Aircraft Procured During World War II

Monocoupe L-7A

A total of 20 Monocoupe 90AFs were procured by the U.S. Government as L-7As. They were powered by the 90 HP Franklin 4-AC-199E3 (O-200-5) four cylinder horizontally opposed engines. They were assigned serial numbers 42-88638 through 42-88657. Serial number 42-88655 was cancelled and the remaining 19 L-7As were to be handed over to the French. But with the downfall of France in May of 1940, the 19 L-7As were delivered to North Africa. They did serve there with the Free French and in support of British troops. They were shipped out of New York City by George Dade, to Britain, and then transferred to North Africa. They were all manufactured by the Monocoupe Company in Orlando, Florida. The Civil Air Patrol (CAP) also used some of the same production run for submarine coastal patrols in the South Eastern United States, but were soon sub-planted by more efficient and larger aircraft with more crew eyes and much longer range and armaments. These were not military L-7As, but stock civilian Monocoupe 90AFs. The wing span was 32 feet, the length was 20 feet, 10 inches, and the wing area was 132.3 square feet. The empty weight was 998 pounds, with a useful load of 640 pounds, giving the L-7A a gross weight of 1600 pounds. The maximum speed was 130 MPH with a cruising speed of 115 MPH. The landing speed was 45 MPH.

Interstate L-8A

It is strange that this aircraft was designated the L-8A when it actually came before the L-6A. The Interstate S1B1, ATC #754, L-8A was practically identical to the Interstate L-6A. Eight of these "Cadets" were ordered and delivered to Bolivian Air Force leaving on November 23, 1942 for LaPaz. The serial numbers were 42-88658 through 42-88665. The engine used was a 65 HP O-170-3—the identical engine used in the L-2s, L-3s, and L-4s. The wing span was 35 feet, 6 inches, the height was 7 feet, 3 inches, and the length was 24 feet. The wing area was 173.8 square feet. The empty weight was 735 pounds with a useful load of 515 pounds with 15 gallons of fuel. The maximum speed was 107 MPH with a cruise speed of 98 MPH and a landing speed of 36 MPH.

Stinson L-9 / O-62

The Stinson L-9s were three-place aircraft, civilian model number 10-A and 10-Bs. The ATC #738 was powered by a Franklin 4AC-199-E3 (O-200-5) four cylinder horizontally opposed air cooled engine. They were almost identical to the earlier Stinson Model 105,

This Interstate is actually an L-8A, after being declared surplus and purchased on the civilian market. The technical name is an Interstate S1B1 Cadet. It is little changed from its military form to civilian form. Note the sloping-out side windows of the cabin for better downward viewing. (AAHS from Charles N. Traslc)

All of the Free French pilots and unit members of G.M.I./11 pose for a photograph. The significance of the females with the infant is unknown. (Jacques Drabier)

the Stinson Model 10 was more refined and much more improved version of the 105 that was introduced several years earlier making its debut in 1939. The 10A was the forerunner of the famous wartime Stinson L-5, and later, the civilian Stinson Voyager 108.

All Stinson L-9s were impressed into military service from the civilian area. Eight of the impressed Stinson Voyager 108s were given the serial numbers 42-88666 through 42-88673. All were powered by the Franklin O-200-1 engine of 90 HP. These eight Stinsons were designated L-9As. Twelve other Voyagers, Model 10As, were also impressed and designated as Stinson L-9Bs. All were powered by the same Franklin engine. The serial were mixed as follows: 42-94130, 42-94136, 42-97051, 42-97430, 42-97432, 42-97434, 42-107278, 42-107406 through 42-107410. All twenty L-9s were turned over to the British Royal Navy. There is also some speculation along with the L-8s. The Stinson L-9s were 21 feet, 8 inches in length, 6 feet, 6 inches in height, and a wing span of 34 feet, with a wing area of 155 square feet. The empty weight was 1010 pounds with a useful load of 677 pounds with 20 gallons of fuel. The maximum speed was 115 MPH.

The Monocoupe 90AF is shown here after the war. The L-7A was identical to this civilian version. The only differences were the fuselage markings, and the insignias. They were all cloth covered and doped. (AAHS)

Ryan L-10

The Ryan L-10 was one of 12 Ryan Model SCW-145s manufactured by the Ryan Aeronautical Corporation with the Civil Aviation Administration (CAA) Approved Type Certificate (ATC) number 658. They were all manufactured at the Ryan facilities on Lindbergh Field at San Diego, California during 1937 and 1938. A single Ryan SCW-145 was impressed into military service and given the designation L-10. It was given the serial number 42-107412, which was originally built as C/N 211, NC18916. It was disposed of by the Army in November of 1944. It was still registered as N46207 in the 1980s. It was powered by the seven cylinder radial air-cooled Warner "Super Scarab" model 50-499 engine developing 145 horsepower. It

There were eight impressed Stinson Voyagers. There are no known photographs of any of the L-9s. This is a photograph of a civilian Voyager shortly after the war in 1947. Note the distinctly family resemblance to the mass-produced Stinson L-5 series. Aft of the door and the wings were all cloth covered. (AAHS)

was enclosed tightly with the small frontal area radial "bump" cowling which was so very popular during that time period.

Bellanca L-11

The L-11 was one of seven Bellanca model 31-50s built in 1935 under the CAA's ATC number 565 and nick-named the Bellanca Senior Skyrocket. It was a six-place high winged aircraft with 180 MPH airspeed, and a 920 mile range with an empty weight of 3150 pounds. Its 56 feet wing span and 28 feet overall length was powered by a 600 HP Pratt and Whitney R-1340-41 nine cylinder air-cooled radial engine. This was one big airplane! It was almost identical to the later built de Havilland of Canada U-1A Otter. This one and only Bellanca model 31-50 was impressed into military service in Alaska, and was given the designation L-11 with the military serial number 42-107421. It was assigned liaison duty on the Canadian Oil Pipeline (CANOL) and the ALCAN highway construction projects in May of 1942. However, it was struck off charge as unairworthy in October of the same year.

Stinson L-12

These were four impressed Stinson Reliants. All were designed by Stinson and built at the Stinson plant in Wayne, Michigan. Two Stinson model SR-5As, nicknamed Model As with ATC number 536, were built in 1935. They were classified as L-12-STs and were two of the famous and popular "Reliant" series powered by the 245 HP Lycoming nine cylinder air-cooled radial R-680-6 engine. The L-12-ST was a four-place high wing airplane with a wingspan of 41 feet, and an overall length of 28 feet, and a height of 9 feet. It cruised at 120 MPH, had a range of approximately 500 miles, and an empty weight of 2325 pounds. Seventy-one were manufactured. These two L-12-STs were impressed into military service in 1944 for use as liaison aircraft. They were given the military serial numbers 44-52994, and 44-52996.

The other two Stinson L-12s were out of eight civilian model Stinson SM-7Bs or Model Bs that were manufactured in 1930 under the CAA's ATC number 329. They were powered by the Pratt and Whitney "Wasp Junior" nine cylinder air-cooled radial engine model R-985A with 300 HP. These two Stinsons were four place high wing airplanes with a wing span of 42 feet and an overall length of 30 feet. It stood 9 feet tall. Empty weight was 2312 pounds and it could cruise at 120 MPH with a range of 550 miles. These two L-12s were impressed during fiscal year 1944 with the designation L-12A-STs. They were given the military serial numbers 44-52992 and 44-52995.

There was only one L-10. It was a Ryan SCW-145, of which only 12 were built. There are no known photographs of the one and only L-10 which was in service with the military for only a short period of time. This photograph shows a SCW-145 at an airshow long after the war. (AAHS)

(Above) *Two of the Stinson L-12s that were pressed into military service, were Stinson SM-7Bs, or Model Bs, that were built in 1930. They were powered by a Pratt & Whitney R-985A engine. There are no known photographs of the L-12, but shown here is a Stinson SM-7B carrying a neon sign, at Parks College in East Saint Louis, Missouri around 1940. (AAHS)*

(Below) *Pilot and instructor, Sgt. Jacques Drabier, kneels beside a Monocoupe 90A of G.M.I./11 "Groupe Desert de Surveillance" of the Free French in Syria in 1943. The rudder colors were red/white/blue. Note the Free French insignia on the fuselage. (Jacques Drabier)*

CHAPTER NINE

Carrier Operations

On November 8, 1942, Operation Torch, the landings in North Africa, began. It was America's first combat test in the European area. They were under the command of General Dwight Eisenhower. The objective was to attack the Germans rear in North Africa.

At dawn on November 9, 1942, three Piper L-4As took off from the U.S. aircraft carrier Ranger, and set course for the Moroccan coast about 60 miles away. As an aid to be recognized by friendly forces, the engine cowlings were painted bright yellow, and the white stars of the national insignia were ringed by a circle using the same bright yellow color. But it was all in vain. All three aircraft come under intense anti-aircraft fire from Allied ships. As a result none of the Pipers reached Morocco, but one was forced down near a Vichy French fort where the crew was taken prisoner, but not for long as the Allies pushed forward and rescued the crew. It was a very inauspicious beginning for combat operations by the U.S. Army aviation.

These were the only known flight operations off of U.S. aircraft carriers by U.S. Army liaison aircraft. But there were other operations off of converted LSTs to mini-aircraft carriers. On top of a standard LST, the Army built its own flight deck about 200 feet long out of plywood. It was about 6 feet above the LST's main deck. About 10 or so Piper L-4s could be carried and

LST-906 loading up the 3rd Infantry Division at Gaetta, Italy on July 31, 1944, is preparing for the invasion of southern France, the "Soft Underbelly Of Europe." The Piper L-4s are on the dock awaiting loading upon the LST. Note the one L-4 on the crane in the air, being hoisted aboard. Also note the plywood "flight deck" built on top of the LST. (National Archives)

Once fully loaded, the "flight deck" of the LST appears to be very crowded, and it is! A careful examination of the Piper L-4s will show that they are all missing their rudders. This was done for clearance reasons for takeoffs and for deck handling. The rudders were very easily re-attached to the L-4 prior to operations of the L-4. (Jim Crow)

(Above) *Not all of the Piper L-4s made a safe landing during the invasion of southern France. Here, "Sad Sack II" is being hauled ashore at St. Tropez, France. The code on the side of the L-4 is BE. BE was the 45th Field Artillery Battalion of the 3rd Infantry Division. (Jim Crow)*

(Below) *This LST is launching more Piper L-4s off the southern coast of France in 1944. Most of the L-4s have been launched, as there are very few left onboard. Another L-4 awaits clearance for takeoff. When an LST maneuvered full speed into the wind for takeoffs, they were steaming along at 8 knots!!! (LST Association)*

A Piper L-4 lifts off the "flight deck" of an LST in the invasion of southern France in the summer of 1944. There are no catapults or cables to catch the tailhook. The flight was a one-way flight—the L-4s could not be recovered on the LST—they had to land on land—albeit sand of the beach, a farmer's field, a pasture, anyplace that was a few hundred feet long, and semi-level. (Jim Crow)

operated off of the LST. These LST flight operations were not used at Normandy's D-Day operations, but they were used very successfully at landing in Sicily and also in southern France invasions. In addition, they were important in the retaking of the Philippine Islands.

The 16 feet wide runway was more than enough for the Piper L-4s to take off into the head wind. It was intended for take-offs only. The aircraft would then land on, and then operate from the beachhead, or road, or rice paddy, sandy beach or any other reasonably flat piece of ground a couple of hundred feet long. The rudders of the L-4s on the side holding ramps of the LST, were removed to make a better clearance for the L-4 taking off on the plywood runway.

This was necessary in order for the wings of the L-4 taking off to clear the planes below. As each L-4 was put onto the runway, the rudder was installed, and the

LST-386 off of Lake Bigerte before the invasion of Sicily in June of 1943, displays the readiness of Piper L-4, 43-1105. A workman is making final preparations at the Licata invasion area. FA on the tail means Fifth Army, not Field Artillery where a lot of Piper C-4s were assigned. (National Archives)

(Above) *These Piper L-4s are onboard LST-525 in August of 1944, prior to the invasion of southern France. They are in a port in Italy. L-4s are from the 36th Infantry Division. L-4 coded DB is from the 131st Field Artillery Battalion of the 36th Infantry Division, but L-4 coded UB is from the 460th Parachute Field Artillery Battalion of the 7th Army. (Tom Hale)*

(Below) *Piper L-4 lands on a dock next to LST-906, so it can be hoisted onto the LST for shipment to the invasion area. (National Archives)*

LST would turn into the wind and come to its maximum speed, some where around 8 to 10 knots if possible. That was sufficient to launch the plane on the 200 feet flight deck. But because of the narrow 16 feet wide runway, and the rolling and pitching of the LST, there were some real fancy rudder actions taking place!

Since the LST carrier operations were so successful in the European Theatre of Operations, it was decided to try them out over in the Pacific area also. So, the LSTs went back to the states, retro-fitted with more L-4s, and sailed to the Pacific, just in time to be used as part of MacArthur's invasion of the Philippines in October of 1944, and later in Lingayan Gulf , but now the slow moving LSTs had to dodge Kamikaze aircraft. No L-4s or LSTs were lost on any Pacific carrier operations.

After the war, with the advent of the helicopter, all LSTs were easily converted back to straight LSTs, and all LST carrier operations and development stopped.

CHAPTER TEN

Gliders

On May 10, 1940, nine German assault gliders carrying 78 specially trained glider troops landed inside the "impregnable" Belgium fortress of Eden Emael. In less than a half an hour, these German assault troops had seized control of this key position manned by almost 800 Belgium soldiers. A new weapon of war had come into play—the glider! The military world suddenly opened its eyes to the advent of a new, and this seemingly potent weapon.

When these swift, silent glider assaults opened the way for the German forces to rapidly advance through Belgium and Holland and on to France without having to make a frontal attack against the Maginot Line, military commanders around the world suddenly realized that a new dimension had been added to combat. This was also noticed by General Hap Arnold, and on February 25, 1941, he directed his staff to prepare a study on the military transport glider.

In April of 1941, Captain Marc Mitchner, Chief of the U.S. Navy's Bureau of Aeronautics, also directed an investigation of a military glider for the Navy and Marine Corps.

In the morning of May 20, 1941, 53 German assault gliders began landing on the island of Crete in the first wave of a massive airborne invasion. British and New Zealand troops were unable to defend the island against airborne warfare with paratroopers, and combat gliders.

In that same month of May of 1941, the Air Corps ordered its first troop transport gliders. Responding were the Frankfort Sailplane Company, Waco Aircraft Company, St. Louis Aircraft Company, and Bowlus Sailplane Company. These companies were civilian sailplane manufacturers, whose designs were similar to light-weight, high performance sailplanes than military troop gliders. Waco won the design with their CG-4A, and a phenomenal total of 13,909 were eventually built.

With glider production ordered in large quantities, it was not without embarrassment that the Army did not know where to get pilots to fly this formidable new air assault weapon.

None of the U.S. military services had any glider pilots nor had they developed any plans for training them by 1941. Therefore, the services started impounding from private owners every two-seat sailplane that could be found, and also began ordering new two-seat sailplanes to equip the as yet to open military glider schools. In 1941, this glider training was so hastily planned that the U.S. Army had only one glider in service, ONE Frankfort XTG-1.

By very early in 1942, it was obvious that the sail plane companies could not turn out enough training

An early production TG-6-TA displays U S Army under the silver-doped wings. The TG-6A was a three-seat training glider version of the Taylorcraft L-2 with an enlarged fin and rudder, wing spoilers added, and a simplified landing gear. (John Conway)

The Taylorcraft TG-6 was a three-seat glider version of the Taylorcraft L-2. The aircraft in the photograph was a one-of-a-kind experiment called the "Glomb"—a glider bomb, with explosives in the nose, and guided to the target by radio control. The Navy program did not work well, at all. Note that the aircraft has no seats in it, an added nose wheel for level loading of the bomb, and under the glass at the nose, various radio controls can be seen. Faintly visible are various antennae on the top of the Glomb. (John Conway)

gliders, and that the Army did not have the instructors or facilities to turn out the required number of pilots to man the coming flood of Waco CG-4As. Army cadets who had trained on the confiscated sailplanes, were experiencing severe problems when transitioning to CG-4As. The CG-4A behaved nothing like the typical high-performance sailplane, with a glide ratio of 25 to 1. The CG-4A was about 8 to 1. It is no wonder that the newly trained pilots were coming to grief when faced with the truck-like CG-4A glider.

Both major problems of the glider programs, (1) not enough glider pilots being turned out, and (2) the existing training sailplanes having no where near the same flight characteristics of the CG-4As, were solved indirectly by one major move. The Army wanted glider pilots trained quickly with a minimum of time and effort. Calculating that a glider pilot's combat life would be less than 6 minutes, it seemed foolish to train

The first Aeronca XTG-5-AE as a three-seat training glider version of the L-3 with a redesigned forward fuselage and triple tandem seats with the instructor in front. The first prototype carried a civilian experimental registration. It was silver doped. (John Conway)

Taylorcraft produced 250 training gliders called TG-6As. All were silver doped. In addition, the U S Navy received 45 TG-6As and designated them as LNT-1s. They were all produced in a very short period of time—only a few months. They were extremely easy to built, and very economical. (John Conway)

him in the same high degree as a future bomber or fighter pilot. After all, he was only expected to know how to get in the air behind the towing aircraft and how to land—once! Therefore, it was decided to use NCOs as pilots, and not commissioned officers.

Therefore, sailplanes were out. The Army pointed out that the landing of a military assault glider was similar to an engine-out forced landing in a conventional-powered aircraft. The Army also noticed that the Waco CG-4A looked like a very large Piper Cub painted Olive Drab, and that the wing loading was also about the same as a Cub. Therefore, they should handle like a Cub. Since the Pipers, Aeronca, and Taylorcraft light planes were cheap, easy to build, and readily available, it was decided that as s stop-gap program, initial glider training would be given in these L-2s, L-3s, and L-4s.

The use of these liaison planes for instruction actually involved no extra items for the student to learn, because all the necessary maneuvers that would be learned for a liaison aircraft are the same for a glider.

Therefore, Aeronca's idea was to remove the engine and cowling, and replacing them with a third seat in a new nose with a tow release. The weight of the 65 HP engine that was removed, was the same as the student that was added, so there was no change in weight and balance. A new, lower landing gear was fitted to give the Aeronca a ground attitude similar to the CG-4A.

The result was a prototype being towed into the air nine days later, and completing all military tests in

The glider version of the Piper L-4 series was called the TG-8-PI with an extended nose, wing spoilers, and a modified landing gear. All of the Pipers were painted with silver dope. Like all of the other liaison-converted-to-glider airplanes, they were mass produced in a very short period of time—only a few months. The military got all that they wanted in a very short period of time at a very economical price. (John Conway)

A camouflaged Stinson L-1 in the foreground, shares the ramp at 29 Palms, California in late 1942, or early 1943, with quite a few Piper TG-8 glider trainers. The gliders were all sprayed with silver dope. With over 13,000 Waco UGC-4 glider ordered, there was a huge demand for glider pilots. These little liaison-converted gliders proved to be just what the military needed, and they worked very well, training thousands of men to be glider pilots. (John Conway)

only 24 days after the go-ahead. The converted Aeronca L-3 became the XTG-5. Maurice Fry flew it for its first flight on May 20, 1942. Additional vertical fin area was added to counter the increased side area of the extended canopy. The prototype initially had a tail-skid, but a tail wheel was fitted.

The TG-5 was a tandem three-seat training glider. Two seats were in the same location as the L-3, while the third seat was in the new nose. All three seats had basic flying controls and instruments. The training flight crew was typically an instructor pilot with two student glider pilots. This allowed for one student to fly while the other observed. Through this two student/one instructor arrangement has been used by several foreign air forces for pilot training, the TG-5, 6, and 8s were the only U.S. military trainers, to use this arrangement. Solo was from the front seat only.

The fuselage of the TG-5 was a welded steel tube structure covered with fabric over spruce fairing stringers. The fuselage was 23 feet, 10 inches long. The wing structure consisted of two solid spruce spars with aluminum alloy ribs. The entire structure was fabric covered. The ailerons had metal frames with fabric covering. With the exception of a spoiler, the wing was identical to that of a L-3 with a span of 35 feet and an area of 169 square feet. The empennage was identical to the L-3 except for an increased area of the vertical fin to balance the longer nose. The TG-5 had a stearable tail wheel like the L-3. TG-5s had a battery and position lights for night gliding. Most were equipped with radios.

The TG-5 had an empty weight of only 635 pounds, and a gross weight of 1260 pounds. The maximum speed was 129 MPH. The best glide speed was 55 MPH, and the stall speed was 46 MPH. As a result of these tests, the U.S. Army ordered 250 TG-5s from Aeronca.

Despite this order, the need for glider training was very urgent, and many more than Aeronca could mass produce were needed. Therefore, Taylorcraft and Piper were asked to modify their L-2s and L-4s in a similar manner. Taylorcraft responded immediately, and the U.S. Army, also ordered 250 of them designated the TG-6.

Piper made a similar conversion from their L-4 and was also awarded a contract for 250 of them that were called TG-8s. It was contract W535ac-31398 valued at $533,435.23 issued on August 19, 1942, and included the three LNP-1s for the U.S. Navy. That is a unit cost of about $2100 each, which is very economical.

All of these TGs were built very quickly in less than six months, and were able to provide the U.S. military with the badly needed training gliders.

Since the training gliders were basically an unpowered light plane, which the students learned to fly in, and was already familiar with, the transition was smooth, and the entire course, including ground school, was only six months.

Student glider pilots first learned to fly in powered light planes like the Piper L-4. By using L-4s, they got in more air work, as they did not have to be constantly re-towed back to altitude. Also the U.S. had fleets of Cubs in civilian pilot training schools in initiate training and could turn out basic pilots by the thousands. After training on power-planes like the L-4, the student pilot then transitioned to the training glider for actual glider operations and tow-line experience.

In 1943, it became apparent to senior Navy planners that troop and cargo assault gliders were not practical for the South Pacific operations. Therefore, On June 24, 1943, the U.S. Navy terminated their glid-

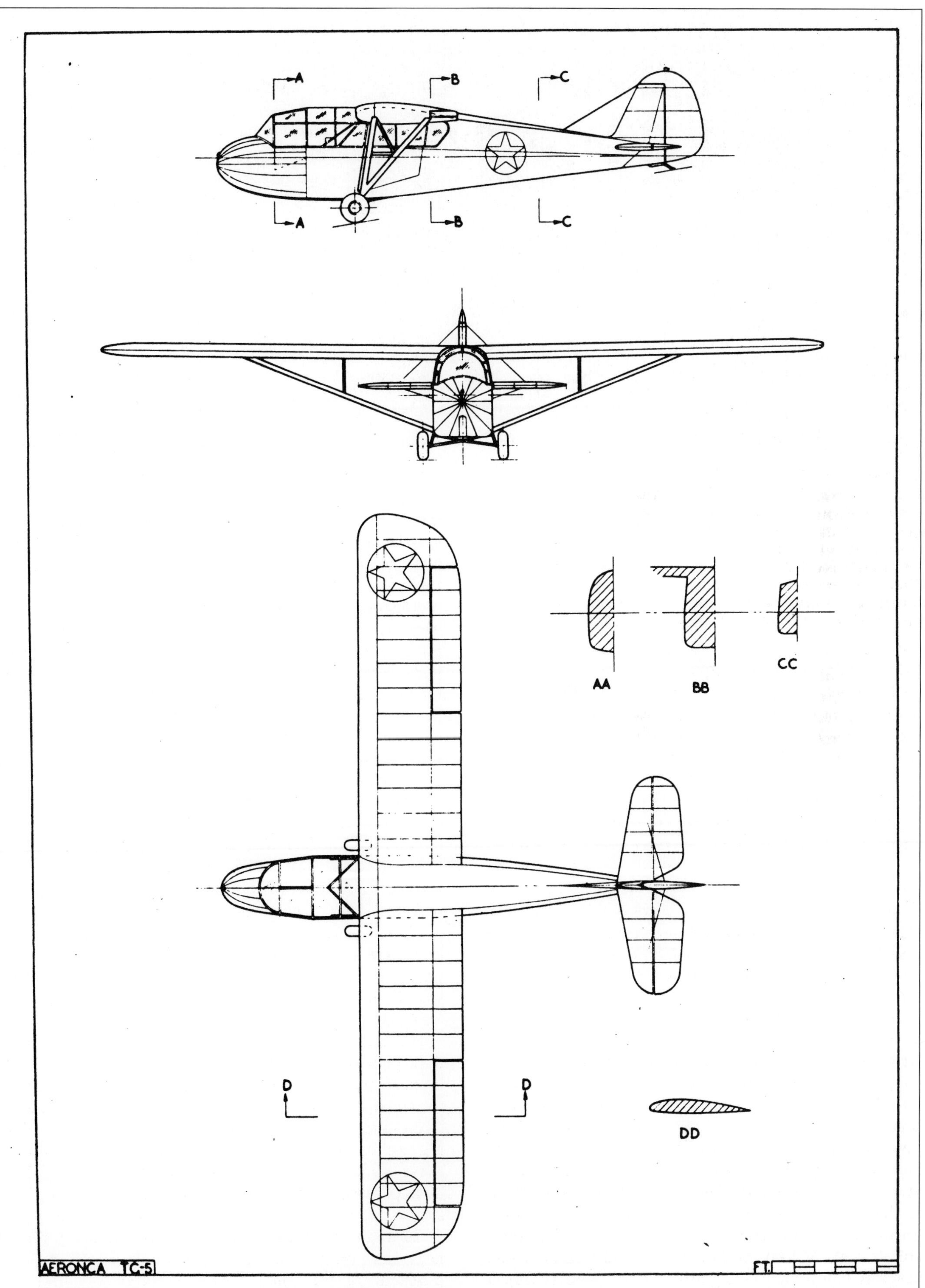

Three view drawing of the Aeronca TG-5 (L-3).

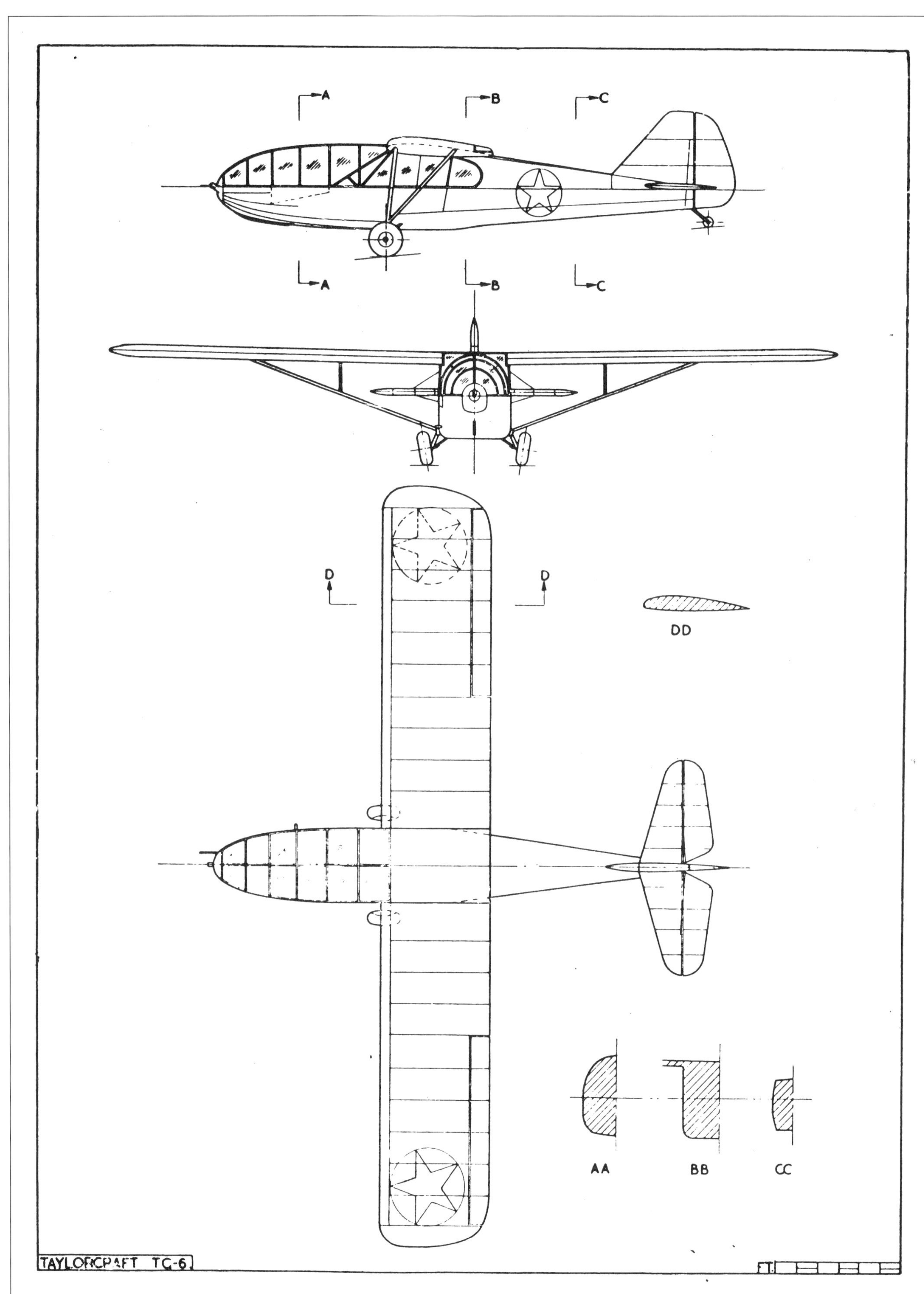

Three view drawing of the Taylorcraft TG-6 (L-2).

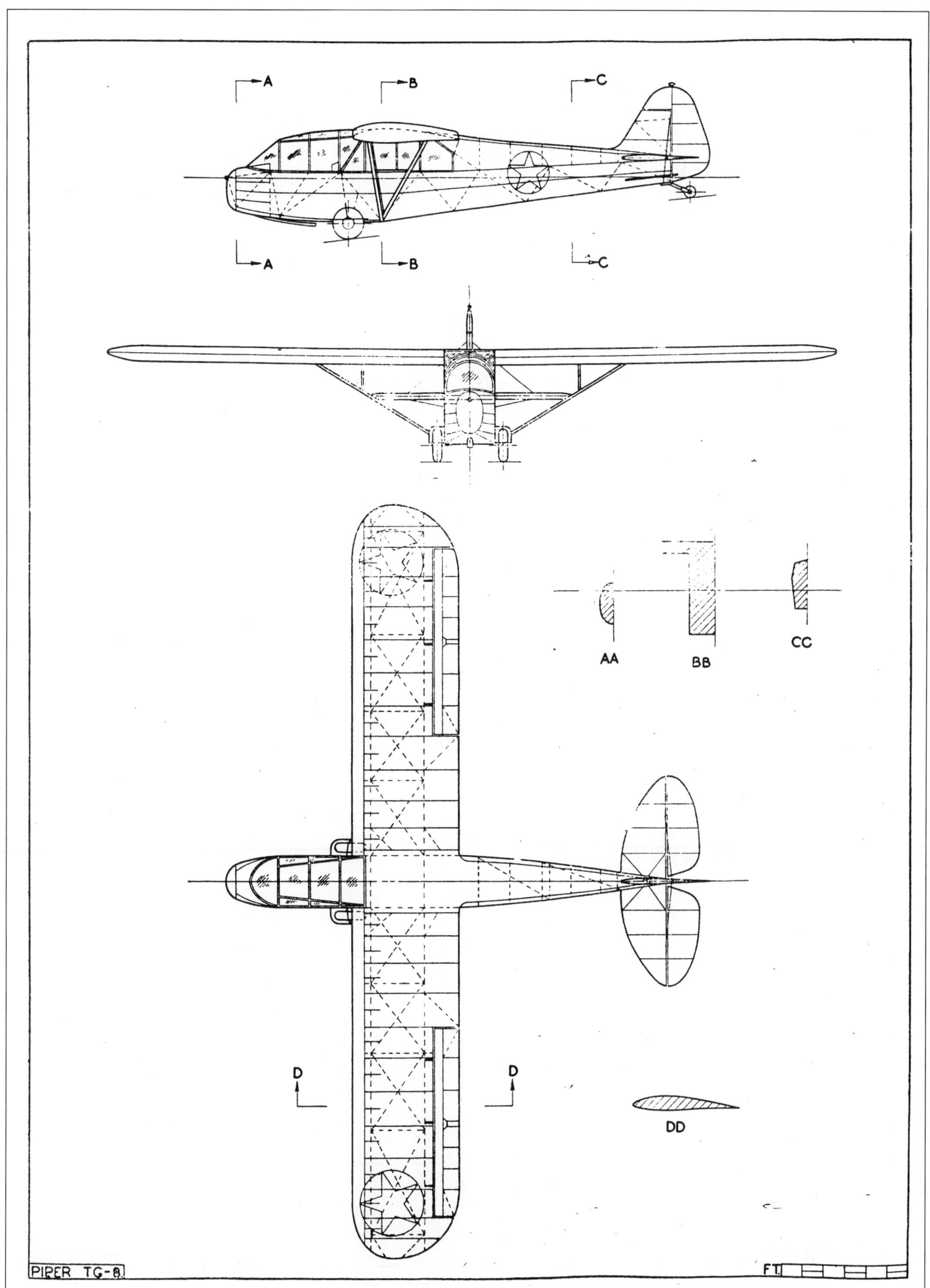

Three view drawing of the Piper TG-8 (L-4).

er programs, and turned them over to the Army.

Large scale glider pilot training came to an abrupt end in early 1944 after more than enough glider pilots had been trained, and the 750 odd number of the three TG types in use were quickly declared surplus. Later many of these were converted into powered aircraft and many are still flying today.

The sergeant pilots, who included in their number former child-actor Jackie Coogan, and cowboy star Gene Autry.

Most of the fully trained glider pilots had been sent to the Mediterranean for the invasion of Sicily or to England for the invasion of France on D-Day.

Several gliders were built as glider bombs and flight tested to deliver the atomic bomb that was being developed at the time. The was a highly classified project at the time. However, with the development of the atomic bomb and the B-29 delivery techniques, further development of the GLOMB (glider-bomb) was unnecessary, and development was terminated.

CHAPTER ELEVEN

Brodie System

When the United States entered World War II, one of the main priorities was the reduction of German submarine attacks on coastal shipping and North Atlantic convoys. The U.S. Navy was unable to provide adequate convoy protection from U-boats and wolf-packs along the convoy's routes. Many ideas were considered which might quickly provide daylight air observation ahead of the convoy, so that all of the U-boats lying in wait on the surface might be detected and the convoy diverted away.

The Brodie system was one such concept to provide air observation for a convoy, by basing liaison aircraft on one or more of the convoy's ships. Lieutenant James H. Brodie, U.S. Army Field Artillery, developed an operable system that could be utilized on a ship, or on land.

By early 1943, in the New Orleans, Louisiana area, Lt. Brodie developed the prototype system, The Brodie System was a device intended to permit the operation of liaison aircraft from ships or from jungle or similarly inhospitable terrain. It consisted of a cable, 500 feet long, and strung between two masts. A "hook" mounted on top of the aircraft permitted the liaison aircraft to takeoff and land while suspended some fifty feet minimum above the ground or ocean surface.

To develop the idea, two rigs were erected at Fort Sill, Oklahoma, and tested. Aside from broken propellers, there were no accidents. To show how simple and easy it was to operate, some top students from pilot graduating classes began to also train on the Brodie System. They soon became so adept at using the Brodie System, that boredom became a problem. One student flew over the rig at 1,000 feet, cut the engine to stop the propeller, and came around and hooked-up deadstick. Another student came over the rig, did a loop and hooked up out of the bottom of the loop. They were grounded for a week, but it illustrated how easy it was to do.

In September of 1943, a ship version was installed on the cargo vessel named City Of Dalhart, and tested in the Gulf of Mexico off the coast of New Orleans, Louisiana. U.S. Army Air Corps Staff Sergeant R. A.

LST-776 was one of four LSTs outfitted with the Brodie System, and the only one that was operational. It was expected to be used for the invasion of Kyushu, Japan, in Operation Coronet, the planned invasion of Japan in November of 1945. The use of the atomic bombs and the surrender of Japan negated the invasion. (LST Association)

Since the Brodie system was a highly classified system during the war, photographs of the structures and operations are very rare. It was used successfully in the Pacific. It was never used for European operations. (LST Association)

Gregory made a series of takeoffs and landings from the ship in his Stinson L-5. However, by that time, the German submarine menace was severely reduced because of the advent of sonar, long-range B-24 patrols, and U.S. Navy convoy escort ships. Therefore, the priority was reduced considerably.

But the possible usefulness of the U.S. Navy ship equipped with the Brodie System to support beachhead landings and the anticipated invasion of Japan, raised the priority again. The Office of Strategic Services (OSS was the forerunner of the CIA,) was organized under Major General "Wild Bill" Donovan to conduct espionage, sabotage, guerrilla warfare, psychological operations and escape and evasion behind enemy lines. The OSS assumed direction of the Brodie System development, and the OSS high priorities accelerated the project for OSS use also. The Brodie system was considered so top-secret that the operation was under the direction of the OSS.

With the flaps lowered, this L-5 is positioning itself for the next mission. This well-weathered L-5 had had its right fuel tank replaced, and a few patches are on the left wing on the "stars and bar." The "full steam ahead" speed of an LST was 8 knots. Not much "wind over the decks" speed, but it worked. (AFM)

Stinson L-5B, 44-16835, receiving an observer as it prepares to launch using the Brodie System method of operations from an LST. The system worked well, although it was not adapted in wide-spread use. (AFM - James Brodie)

After the system was perfected, OSS, Navy, and Army high ranking officers viewed the system, and approved continuance of the program. In June of 1944, the Navy authorized a Brodie System installation on LST-776, and Brodie, Sergeant Gregory, and staff proceeded to the Navy's Amphibious Training Base at Coronado, near San Diego, California. By September, they had trained Navy personnel on the LST how to use the system.

The ship-board system differed form the land system only in the fact that the runway was about 300 feet instead of 500 feet, and the runway cable was suspended by booms outboard of the LST. Landing techniques on the LST were similar to that of the land rig except the added thrill of handling the roll of the LST, which was notorious with its round bottom hull.

Ship operations were then begun using Piper L-4s and Stinson L-5s off of San Diego. The ship's forward motion directly into the prevailing wind reduced the need for a longer cable, because the 300 feet long cable on the LST was ample for take-off. The L-5 had a starter on the engine. However, the L-4 had to be "propped"—a little difficult 50 feet above the ocean. But thanks to the L-4s large side door opening, the pilot could climb out with one foot on the landing gear strut, and hand-start the engine.

In March of 1945, using a U.S. Army Field Artillery pilot, LST-776 liaison aircraft flew fire-direct missions for twenty-four 155mm howitzers of Keisa Shima, eight miles from Okinawa. The artillery support made the initial beach-head landings at Okinawa a success.

During the summer of 1945, LST-776 was located in Manila Bay, training additional Army liaison pilots for the planned invasion of Japan.

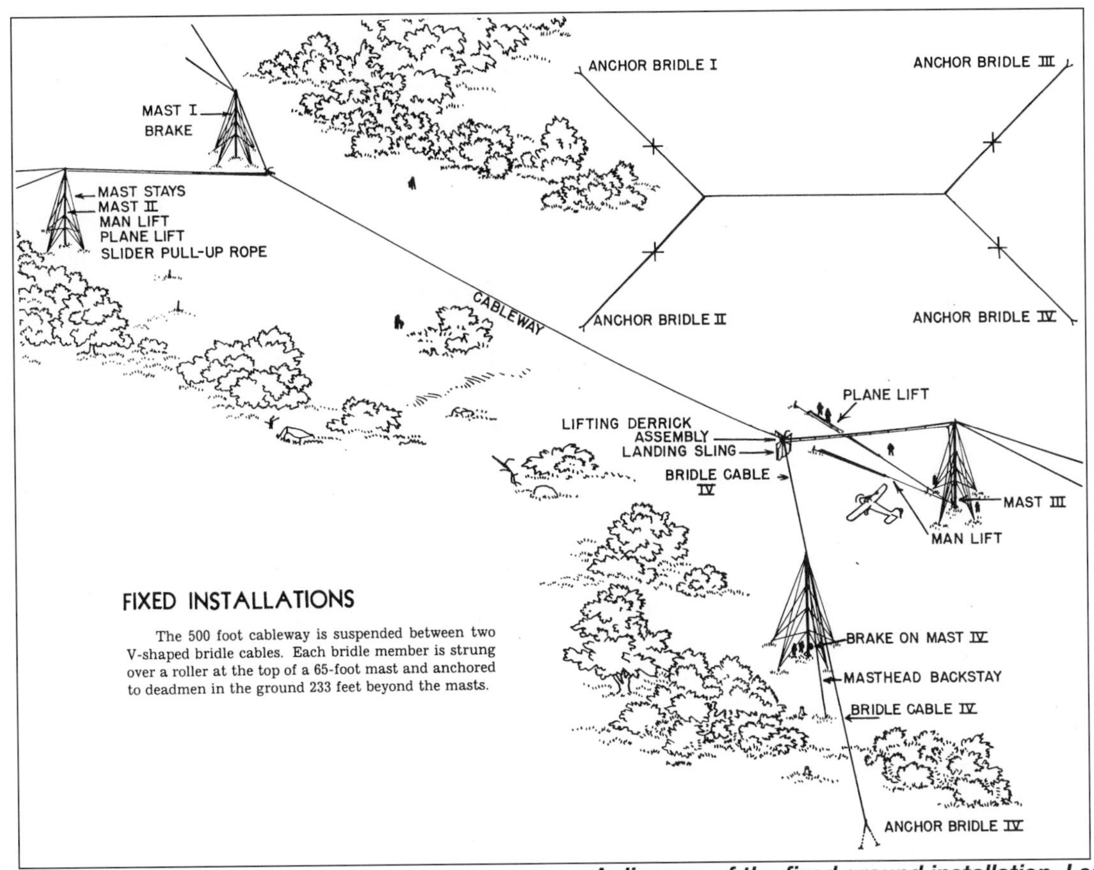

A diagram of the fixed ground installation. Less than 9000 lbs, it could be air-dropped into unimproved terrain. Required crew of nine. (OSS Presentation - James Brodie)

Earlier in November of 1944, some U.S. Army and OSS personnel went to India to erect a land-rig Brodie System and demonstrate its operation to the British. They erected it at RAF airbase at Jessore, India. This RAF base supported several secret, clandestine activities. One example was dropping trained nationals of Japanese-occupied countries (like Burma) into these territories, where they directed guerrilla activities.

The British liked the system—both land and ship versions. The ship versions were planned to be installed on the sides of two British hospital ships operating along the coast of Burma. This would permit seriously-wounded personnel to be transported by British L-5s from forward combat airstrips in Burma directly to the hospital ships of the coast. In as much as the Japanese forces were by that time, rapidly withdrawing from Burma, the plan was dropped.

However, in actual use, the system was used little, except at Okinawa from an LST that was Brodie equipped. Four other LSTs were being converted to the Brodie system for the invasion of Kyushu, Japan. The war ended before they were needed.

The Brodie System was not used in Europe, either for D-Day landings or subsequently. However, one Brodie rig sample was sent to England for evaluation

The pilot and observer climbed out, and then lowered themselves onto the L-5. Luckily, the L-5 had a starter on the engine. Then the LST steamed into the wind for launch, like an aircraft carrier. The L-5 then flew down the wire, and lifted off on its mission. (AFM - James Brodie)

by the Royal Aircraft Establishment at Farnborough, but tests were not impressive for European use, but were ideal for use by the British in Burma, and India where airfields were rare, and clear, level land for airfield ever rarer. But by early 1945, the Burma Road was practically open, the Japanese were retreating, and, therefore, the Brodie system was utilized by the British very little for their operations in Burma.

However, the Brodie System was used successfully by the U.S. Army during the fight for Okinawa. Only Piper L-4s and Stinson L-5s for the system.

Upon the Japanese surrender, all Brodie system programs were terminated. With the rapid advancement of the helicopter, the Brodie system was never used again by U.S. military services.

(Above) ***This Piper L-4 is being prepared for a mission offshore of the Kerama Tettas Islands, which can be seen in the background, on March 29, 1945. "Propping" or starting the engine of an L-4 50 feet above the water, could be "interesting" since the pilot had to stand out on the wing strut and pull sharply to fire the engine. Luckily most pilots are not scared of heights. (AFM - James Brodie)***

(Below) ***LST-776, underway at sea, displays the operational equipment of the Brodie System with Stinson L-5, 42-98268 "on the wire." Pilots became very adept at "hooking the wire." (James Brodie)***

CHAPTER TWELVE

1st Air Commando Group

During World War II, the Army Air forces organized three special groups designated Air Commando Groups. Undoubtedly the most famous of these units was the 1st Air Commando Group (1st A. C. G.), which was organized on March 25, 1944, and activated at Hailakandi, Asansol, India where it was based until after the end of hostilities. The first commander was Col. Philip G. Cochran, who was picked by General Hap Arnold. Col. Cochran was the prototype for Flip Corkin, one of the heroes in Milton Caniff's "Terry and the Pirates" comic strips. The second commander was Col. Clinton B. Gaty from May 20, 1944 until Col. Robert W. Hall took over on April 7, 1945. The unit was attached to the Tenth Air Force on July 10, 1945. The unit was inactivated on November 3, 1945. It was later re-activated on April 18, 1962 as part of TAC (Tactical Air Command).

Squadrons of the 1st A.C.G. included the 5th Fighter Squadron, 6th Fighter Squadron, 164th Liaison Squadron, 165th Liaison Squadron, and the 319th Special Operations Squadron (airlift).

The unit was comprised of operational sections, rather than units until reorganized in September of 1944. Operational sections included 12 bombers (B-25s), 33 fighters (P-51s and P-47s), and 103 liaisons (L-1s and L-5s), transports (10 UC-64s and 13 C-47s), gliders (150 CG-4As and 25 TG-5s), and 3 helicopters (YR-4s).

The group provided fighter cover, bomb striking power, and air transport support for Wingate's Raiders and Merrill's Marauders, operating behind enemy lines in Burma.

Operations included airdrops and landing of troops, food, and equipment, medical evacuations, and attacks against enemy airfields and lines of communication.

The fighter squadrons started out with P-51As, and converted to P-47Ds and eliminated the B-25s by the summer of 1944. The group also continued performing support services for other allied forces in Burma until the end of the war. They also attacked bridges, railroads, airfields, barges, oil wells, and troops in Burma and escorted bombers to Burmese targets, including Rangoon. They traded in their P-47s for P-51Ds in May of 1945.

The Group markings were five white, diagonal, this stripes on the fuselage. They had many firsts including the first military use of an American helicopter, the Sikorski YR-4 (only 30 were built.) By April of 1944, the YR-4 was in Burma. Lieutenant Carter Harman was flying the YR-4 into the steamy jungles of northern Burma. Lt. Harman flew into a secret outpost behind Japanese lines in those Burmese jungles. At this outpost, American forces were supporting British raiders who were trying to re-open the Burma Road so supplies could get to China. Lt. Harman was ordered to pluck out a downed American pilot and three British casualties from the jungle 30 miles away. The American, flying an Stinson L-1, had been bringing the British out when engine trouble forced them down. With no landing strip within many miles, the four men were doomed.

Lt. Harman found them in his YR-4, but he had a problem. The altitude, humidity, and heat had thinned the air, sharply reducing the engine's power and the rotor blades' lifting capacity. Harman knew that his YR-4 could barely hover with only himself on board. But he had to try to rescue them. With one of the injured British beside him in the cabin, Harman gunned the engine, revving his rotor to the limit, and pulled up on the collective pitch lever. The YR 4 rose about 20 feet in the air. Then Harman nosed forward to pick up forward speed and flew away. Miles away, he unloaded the wounded Englishman in a dried-out riverbed from which a Stinson L-5 could land and fly him out to a hospital. After the second trip out with another wounded Englishman, the engine became so dangerously overheated that h e had to stop for the day, but he returned the next morning for the last two soldiers. This was the first known combat med-evac mission by helicopter—the first of thousands to follow.

The training gliders, because of their role, were for the most part confined to use within the continental United States. The exception was the use of 25 Aeronca TG-5s by the 1st Air Commando Group in Burma. Except for big European operations such as D-Day and Operation Market Garden in Holland, most combat glider activities took place in Burma.

The 1st A.C.G. provided air support for the invasion of Burma by British forces. Col. Cochran came up with the idea of flying the British troops commanded by British Major General Orde C. Wingate in gliders deep into the heart of Burma. Previously Wingate and Merrill had gone into the bush by foot or raft along rivers. U.S. glider pilots were able to keep Japanese forces off balance, preventing them from invading India.

CHAPTER THIRTEEN

25th Liaison Squadron

Liaison pilots wore an "L" on their wings and flew light planes as artillery spotters, message carriers, and the like. Many of these pilots had washed out of regular pilot training and "retreaded" to fly the puddle-jumpers. Other had private pilots licenses or trained from scratch in military liaison aircraft. There were numerous Liaison Squadrons in the Army Air Forces. One of them, the 159th Liaison Squadron, Commando, whose commanding officer was Captain Rush Limbaugh II, the father of Rush Limbaugh III, famous radio talk-show host and commentator.

One of the most decorated and remembered group of liaison pilots were in the 25th Liaison Squadron, also known as the Guinea Short Lines. They had 125 sergeant pilots. When the 25th arrived in Australia in 1943, they had brought with them everything they needed to operate. Everything that is, except plans or directives from commanders specifically outlining the role of the squadron, and the L-5s they would operate. Therefore, since no one knew what to do with them, the 25th was assigned to the far end of an Australian airfield where they waited and fielded jokes about whether this was a new bomber wing or a new secret weapon. Finally, they were dispatched to New Guinea.

New Guinea was perhaps the most unlikely place for a Liaison Squadron to operate. The small L-5s were designed to takeoff and land from roads, beaches, or fields. New Guinea was mostly jungle. The few clearings found were covered with grass from five to fifteen feet high growing over swamps. It was very unlikely that the L-5s could even operate , but operate they did and very successfully at that!

A line-up of quite a few Stinson L-5s, and all of them have the words "Guinea Short Lines" in a small arc over the kangaroo. This was the squadron logo and saying. Usually on the right side of the cowling, some form of nose art was carried. Since some of the tails are painted white, this photograph was probably taken in the Philippines at Clark Field in early 1945. (Tom Hale)

"The Guinea Short Lines" was the pioneer liaison squadron of the Army Air Forces, that was originally deployed to New Guinea in November of 1943. The unit was so much in demand with the advancing island campaign, that it was reassigned from the 5th Air Force, to answering directly to Headquarters, 13th Air Force. Shown here is a soldier in New Guinea with the beginnings of nose art on the right side of the engine cowling of this Stinson L-5. (Tom Hale)

When a bomber pilot went down, an L-5 pilot volunteered to look for him. The pilot was found and immediately a new rescue was also found for the 25th. The sergeant pilots in their slow and low flying aircraft, could find downed pilots and planes, which would be missed by faster flying, more powerful planes.

One of the most remembered rescues was that of P-47 pilot Captain H. L. McMullen.

McMullen was forced down near Saidor, New Guinea and was spotted by another allied attack bomber who summoned an L-5. Sergeant James Henkle took off from his base St. Saidor, refueled his L-5 along the way, and flew to the Ramu Valley, the scene of bloody fighting and the area where McMullen had crashed. But, search as he did, Henkle could not locate McMullen. On the way back to his base, Henkle encountered bad weather and was forced out to sea, using only dead reckoning. Henkle managed to find the coast and his base with very little fuel left. When he tried again the next day, the same thing happened, and McMullen still had not been found.

Officers of the 25th Liaison Squadron discuss things over a map on the hood of a Jeep, in front of the headquarters tent. Things were primitive in the jungle, but the squadron was equipped with the Stinson L5, and that was a very rugged aircraft that could "live" in the field. (Tom Hale)

The operations had begun on May 23rd, and on May 25th , an intelligence report said signs of prisoners of war had been discovered in the area of the Ramu Valley. A trap was feared, so when Henkle resumed the search the next day, he was accompanied by Sergeant L. E. Gleason on his wing in another L-5 and a fighter squadron flew protection from above.

This time the liaison pilots managed to locate the downed pilot who had been busy clearing an area for the L-5s to land. But, the work had gone slowly and the landing strip was not quite large enough. So supplies were dropped to McMullen and the L-5s scouted the area around him for the enemy. Only a mile or so away, several dark strange looking creatures were spotted dancing and moving into a clearing. It was discovered later that these were Sikha from India who had been taken prisoners by the Japanese and moved to New Guinea, where they were forced into slavery. The

Five pilots of the 25th Liaison Squadron "The Guinea Short Lines", pose for a photograph in front of a squadron Stinson L-5. All of the pilots have their Mae West life jackets on. Note in the background, there is a wrecked Japanese aircraft. (Tom Hale)

Part of the utility of the Stinson L-5, was that it was also a medical evacuation aircraft, able to get into and out of very small areas. Here a 25th Liaison Squadron L-5 brings another patient to an awaiting ambulance for medical attention. The kangaroo insignia comes from the days that the squadron was stationed in New Guinea, very near Australia. Their were a lot of Australian military in the area. (Tom Hale)

Most U S Army Air Force squadrons had squadron "hacks" that were liaison aircraft - like the Piper L4 or the Stinson L-5. However, not the 25th Liaison Squadron, since their flight equipment WAS the Stinson L-5. Apparently the 25th had a Cessna Bobcat as a squadron "hack" as shown here. Date and location are unknown, but it appears to be very warm like New Guinea or the Philippines. (Tom Hale)

Sikhas had escaped and had valuable information on Japanese strengths and movements to furnish to allied troops.

The Sikhas had set up a message pick-up rig by running a line between two poles above the ground. After some investigation, Henkle decided to attempt a pick-up and brought back information outlining specific Japanese movements and bases which the allies used immediately to blowup trails and disrupt Japanese operations.

The next few days Henkle and other L-5 pilots shuttled in medical supplies, food, water, and other equipment to the Sikhas. Then when the Indians found McMullen's airstrip, a rescue shuttle was set up using several L-5s. One by one, the Indians were removed. All in all, 237 of them survived, thanks to the efforts of the men of the 25th.

A pre-war marked Stinson 0-49/L-1 spreads its very large wings. With a 51-foot wing span containing large flaps, and full span slats, the stalling speed was a very low 31 MPH. (Fred Huston)

While the 25th became known as a crazy, rogue bunch who operated at their own will, their services were invaluable as a means of rescue effecting many rescues of downed pilots and stranded units.

When an L-5 spotting plane discovered a Japanese radio position, where there was supposed to be no Japanese at Wantoat, New Guinea, the L-5s were dispatched to ferry in 50 battle hardened Australian commandos and all of their equipment including food, supplies, mortar and other weapons and ammunition. The Australians, known for their hatred of the Japanese, and the ruthless ways in which they operated, succeeded in silencing the radio and wiping out the contingent of Japanese. Four enemy soldiers were taken prisoner and ferried out in the L-5s. Each prisoner was placed on the lap of an Australian commando in the L-5's rear seat with a knife at his neck. There were no attempts at escape.

The 25th was later transferred to the Philippines to support the operations of General MacArthur's liberation of those islands. The commanding officer of the 25th Liaison Squadron was Capt. George Wilson.

CHAPTER FOURTEEN

Foreign Liaison Aircraft — British

Taylorcraft Aeroplanes Ltd. was established at Britannia Works, Leicester, in May of 1939 by English industrialist A. Lance Wykes, an ex-RFC pilot from World War I. He was very impressed with the Taylorcraft. He imported one, and called it an Model A. He received a license, and began producing his first aircraft, which he called an improved Model B, or a Plus C. The first flight was on May 3, 1939. These models used an American engine at first. However, one Taylorcraft was modified to take a Blackburn "Cirrus" Minor engine, due to the anticipation of the war was to begin soon, and the unavailability of American powerplants. This aircraft became the prototype for all Austers produced later. Only 23 pre-production aircraft had been built when the war began on September 3, 1939. These pre-production aircraft were modified to become Plus C-2 or Model Ds. They were in service with the RAF in very small numbers in France prior to the Dunkirk evacuation.

The Plus C had a 55 HP Lycoming engine, and was used for communication duties by the RAF. They were later modified to take the Cirrus Minor engine.

The British Army used the Model D with a 90 HP Cirrus Minor engine for artillery spotting work, which were called Air Observation Posts or AOPs.

The models A through D were mainly limited pre-production experimental models.

The British military had the same thoughts in the late 1930s, on Army artillery spotting and liaison aircraft as the American Army. The British developed the Westland Lysander, but, like the Curtis Owl, it was too fast (315 MPH), too big (50 feet wing span), and too powerful (a 900 HP British Bristol Mercury XII), to be an effective liaison type of aircraft. The Lysander, nicknamed the "Lizzie," had good short field take-off and landing characteristics, and was very rugged. Therefore, it was more towards the right direction of aircraft than the Curtis 0-52 Owl. The versatility of the Lysander made it a much more capable aircraft than the forgettable Owl.

Tests and trials conducted by the British Army in 1940 were witnessed by the U.S. Army's Chief of Artillery. He was suitably impressed and returned to America to persuade his superiors of the potential value of liaison aircraft.

The success of the Taylorcraft led to larger production. The Auster I was the first fully militarized Taylorcraft, and 100 were built. They entered service with No. 651 Squadron in July of 1941, and later with No. 652 Squadron, RAF. They went to North Africa, where it was found to be a little underpowered in that hot climate. Therefore, an American Lycoming 0-290 with 125 HP was installed. It was called the Auster II, but only two were built due to the shortage of the American engine.

The next production variant was the Auster III. It was powered by the De Havilland Gypsy Major, 130 HP engine, giving a top speed of 130 MPH, and a range of 250 miles. There were 467 Auster IIIs built.

The next production model was the Auster IV of which 255 were built. It was powered by the 130 HP Lycoming engine, since, by this time (1943), it was available again from America. The Auster IV had a third seat in it, also.

The following production version was the Auster V, of which 790 were built using the American Lycoming 0-293-3 engine, since by then, 1943, American supply lines were flowing freely across the Atlantic Ocean to England. The Auster V had a blind-flying panel modification. The last Auster V was delivered on January 15,1946. At that time, they changed the company name to Auster Aircraft Ltd. The last production model was the Auster AOP IX powered by a Blackburn "Cirrus" engine of 180 HP.

The Austers served in all theatres of operations and with most Commonwealth countries. Austers also served in Korea and in Malaysia.

After the war was over in Europe, there were a lot of surplus airplanes around. One of the most popular ones for the British, was the Auster AOP. The AOPs were very, very cheap, and cost very little to operate. So they were purchased by the hundreds, and many still survive today as very authentic "warbirds." The Auster AOPs were readily converted to the civilian market. They were easily "de-militarized," since they were basically an "off the shelf" airplane to begin with. Parts are very easy to come by, and the very economical to fly and enjoy.

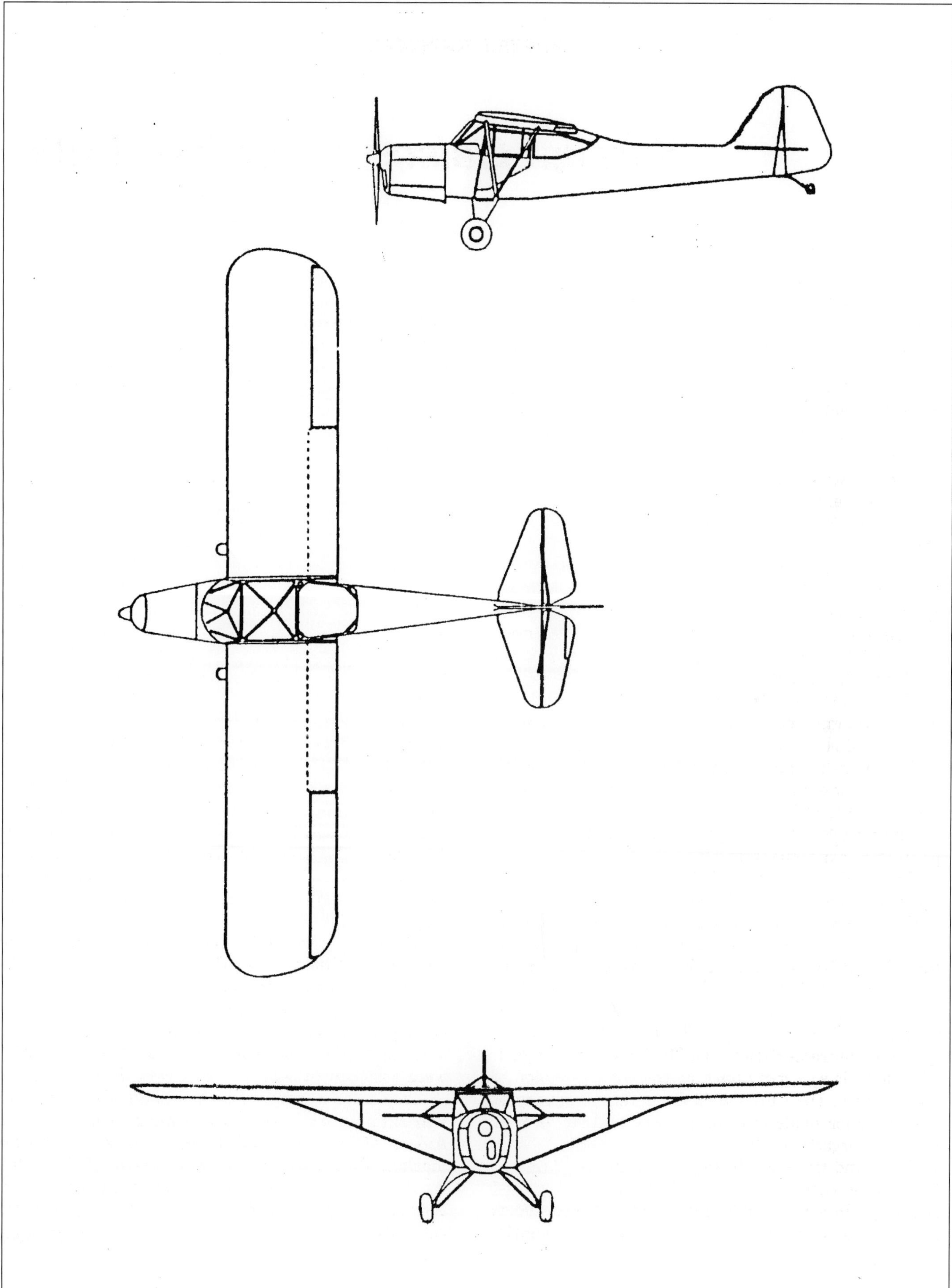

Auster AOP

CHAPTER FIFTEEN

Postwar Liaison and Korea

When North Korea invaded South Korea in June of 1950, there were two U.S. infantry divisions stationed in Korea. Generic to them were quite a few L-4s and L-5s. They assumed a schedule of dawn-to-dusk aerial observation of the retreat and North Korean advances. These L-4s and L-5s were war-weary from World War II five years earlier, and were now nursed into the air for mission after mission. Everything was in short supply including such luxuries as aviation fuel. Therefore, truck and jeep gas again served as a substitute just as it did in the critical days following D-Day in Normandy.

Spare parts for the L-4s and L-5s were non-existent. All repairs were improvised. Some of these included using gas tanks that were stripped from wrecked jeeps and installed in the rear of the L-4s for longer flight times. But in spite of these obstacles, the Army planes continued their low and slow flights over the battle zones, directing accurate and devastating artillery fire on the enemy. Every branch of the service used liaison aircraft in missions ranging from carrying the mail to the evacuation of the wounded.

Army Aviation was a basic part of General Douglas MacArthur's amphibious invasion of Inchon, Korea in September of 1950. In one instance, an Army Captain took off in his L-5 to fly to Kimpo Airfield near Seoul. He was forced to return, however, when he found the airfield in enemy hands. The location he returned to was an aircraft carrier off the coast of Inchon. During the following two months of fighting, the Army lost only six liaison aircraft and one pilot and one observer.

In July 1950, the US Air Force decided to use their L-5s for fighter-bomber direction. The USAF L-5 pilots were trained by Army Aviation pilots. The USAF operations were named "Mosquito." The USAF used observers from the US Army. The L-5 "Mosquito" would be later supplanted by the North American T-6.

Since most of Army Aviation aircraft were well worn L-4s and L-5s. a replacement was sorely needed, and that became the Cessna L-19/O-1 Birddog, which was built by the thousands. The Army had an increasingly urgent need for a modern fixed-wing, two-placed

The U S Navy took delivery of 458 Stinson L-5s, L-5Bs, and L-5Es. They were designated OY-1s, but all retained their Army serial numbers. This is actually 42-98168, on March 15, 1951. The vast majority of the Navy OY-1s went to the Marines, but a very small number went to the U S Coast Guard. (Leo Kohn)

observation and liaison aircraft to replace the obsolete L-4 and L-5 vintage aircraft that were left over from World War II.

On February 16, 1951, the first Cessna L-19 Birddog was delivered to front line units in Korea. The arrival of the new liaison aircraft brought a replacement for the beaten L-4s and L-5s which were replaced on a one-for-one basis. For the experienced Grasshopper pilots, stepping into an L-19 for the first time was like driving a Cadillac after years on a farm tractor. The L-19 was ordered in such large quantities that the unit cost dropped to almost $13,000!

From July 4, 1950 through December 31, 1951, liaison L-4 and L-5s of the U.S. Eighth Army flew 186,372 hours for flying during 140,792 missions. Of these missions, 64,541 were combat sorties. Over 90% of all UN artillery fire was adjusted by L-4 and L-5 aircraft. Also

One of the many Stinson L-5s taken over by the Navy for the Marines, is L-5, serial 42-98197. The color was Marine green over neutral gray. The gray was on the fuselage only. This appears to be a training aircraft, since it has a large number 5 on the fuselage, and no other markings. (Minnesota Air Guard Museum)

during this period, only 10 planes were lost in action, while non-combat accidents reached 122, mainly due to the weather. By 1952, the Cessna L-19 had taken over most liaison missions.

In 1952, Army liaison aircraft flew 117,593 administrative missions, evacuated 7,654 sick and wounded soldiers. Ten pilots were killed in action and two were missing in action.

Piper L-4J, 45-55233, is outwardly identical to the civilian Piper J-3 Cub. It is shown here on Edo 1320 floats. The single rudder on the left float was a standard installation. The location of this 1949 photograph is unknown. It was assigned to the Civil Air Patrol. (author)

(Above) *This Stinson L-5E was given to the Republic of Korea Air Force. K-127 is shown here at K-46 Air Base or Wonju, South Korea on August 15, 1953, shortly after the war was over. (Charles N. Trask via author)*

(Below) *Stinson L-5, serial 44-17087, stands ready for the next mission. These rugged airplanes operated mostly off of dirt and grass strips. The aircraft is silver doped with a flat black anti-glare panel in front of the cockpit. Location is unknown, but probably in the States. (Leo Kohn)*

(Above) *Stinson L-5, serial number 42-98633, went on to serve with the U S Air Force. The Air-Sea Rescue Sentinel has a yellow with black outline strip on the fuselage and most of the wing surface, lower and upper. The rest of the aircraft is silver doped. (Jim Mesko)*

(Below) *Stinson L-5E, serial number 44-18190, in Korea in the early 1950s, was flown by the U S Air Force in the air ambulance mission. Note the section aft of the cockpit which has panels that are moveable to allow the stretcher to be put onboard. The tires on the aircraft are slightly over-sized for really rough-field operations. (Tom Hale)*

(Above) *Stinson L-5E, 44-18198, at Decatur, Illinois on June 11, 1950, belongs to the U S Air Force. The fixed wing slots are clearly visible on the wing's leading edge. The aircraft is painted overall is silver dope, the standard of the time. (Leo Kohn)*

(Below) *U S Air Force Stinson L-5s dot the landing strip at Miryang, South Korea on August 28, 1950. The airfield was supporting the U S 2nd Infantry Division at the time. (Tom Hale)*

Every branch of the service used liaison aircraft in missions ranging from carrying the mail to the evacuation of the wounded to carrying hot meals!

A Piper L-4 is "propped" or started on a dirt road in Korea in 1952 in preparation for a mission. The L-4s easily adapted to the climate and mission in Korea, but there were very few of them left in the inventory, and parts were hard to come by, since they were all being phased out, and replaced by the Cessna L-19 Birddog. (NASM)

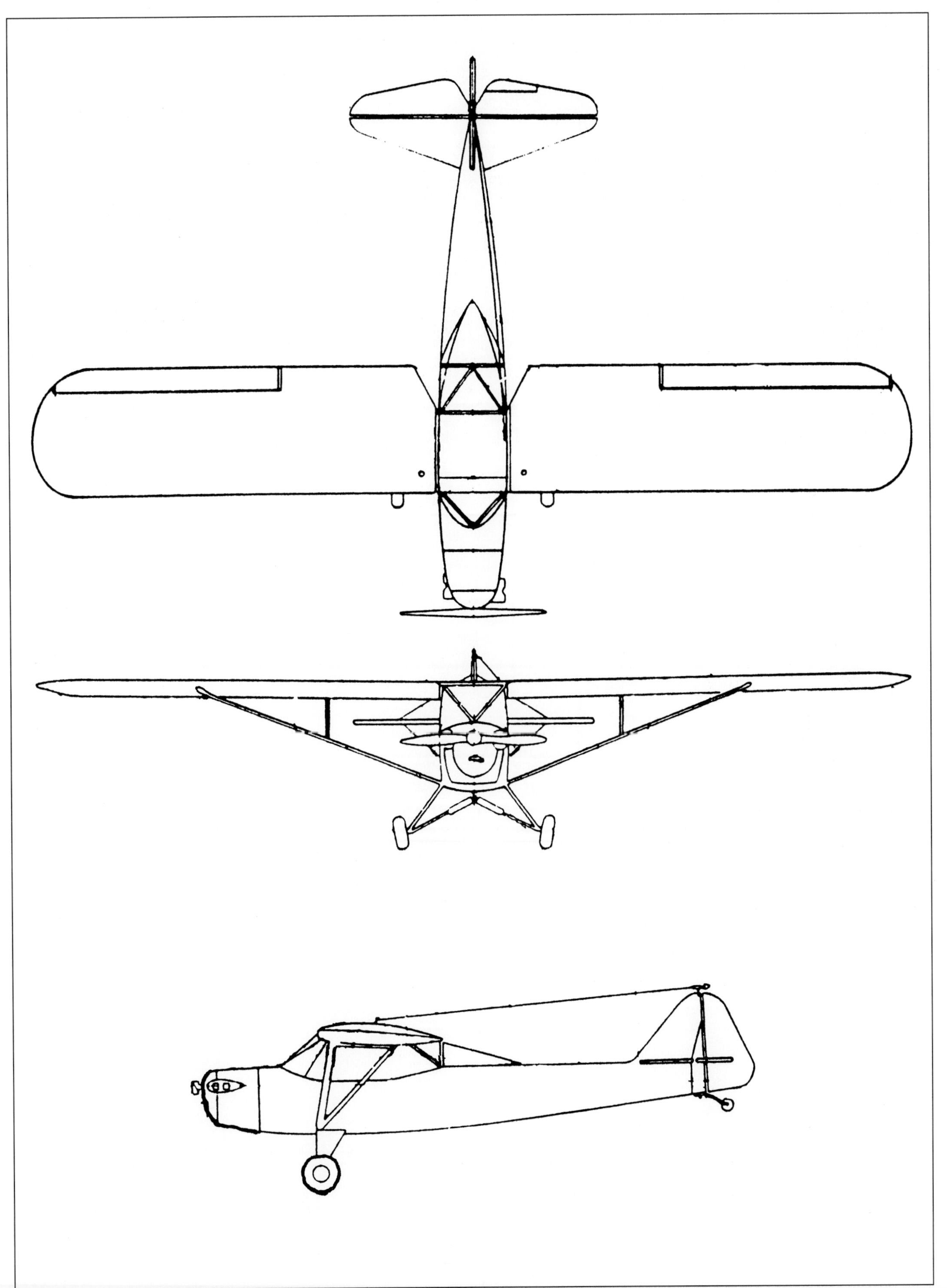

O-57 / L-2

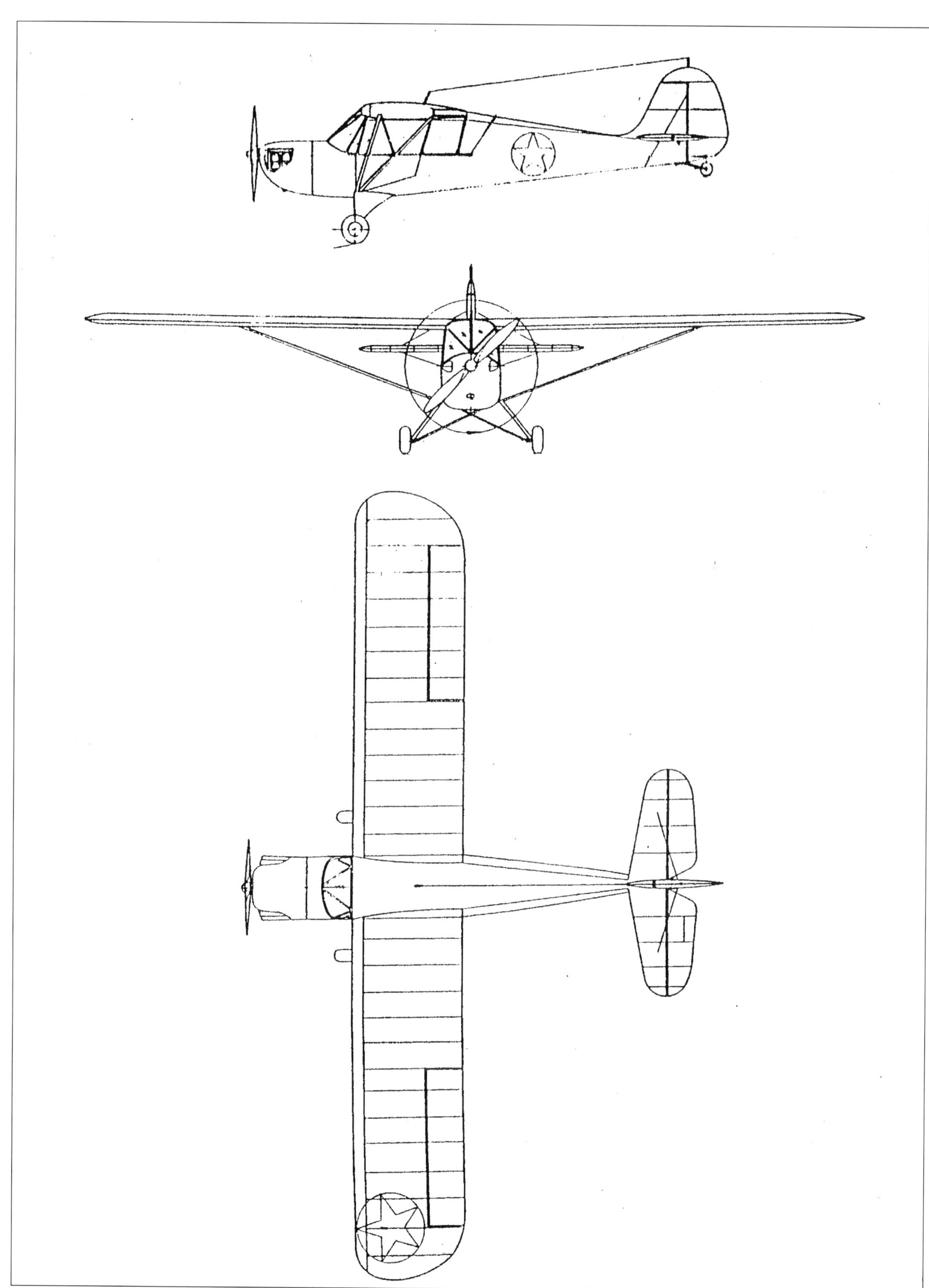

O-58 / L-3

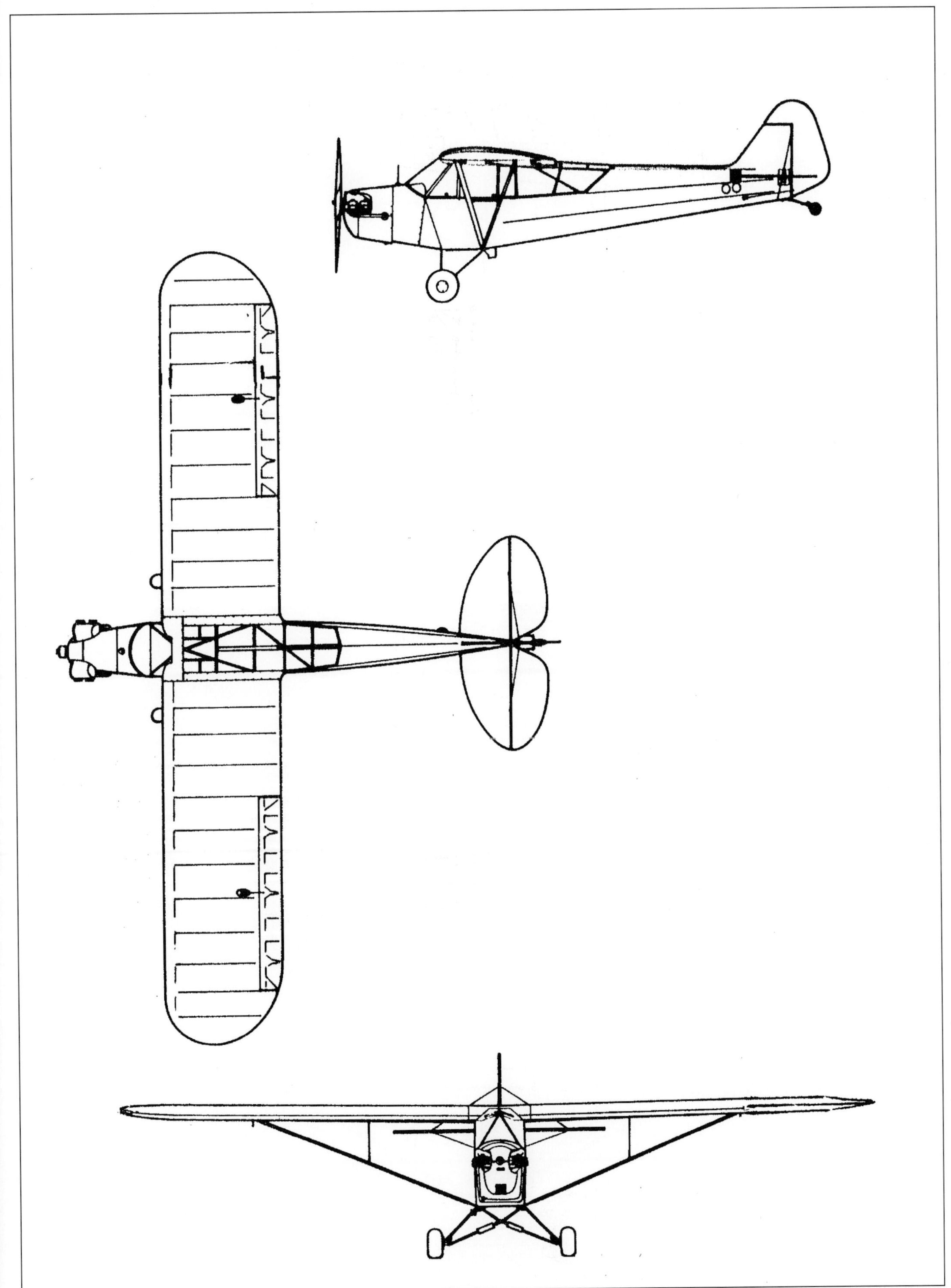

O-59/L-4

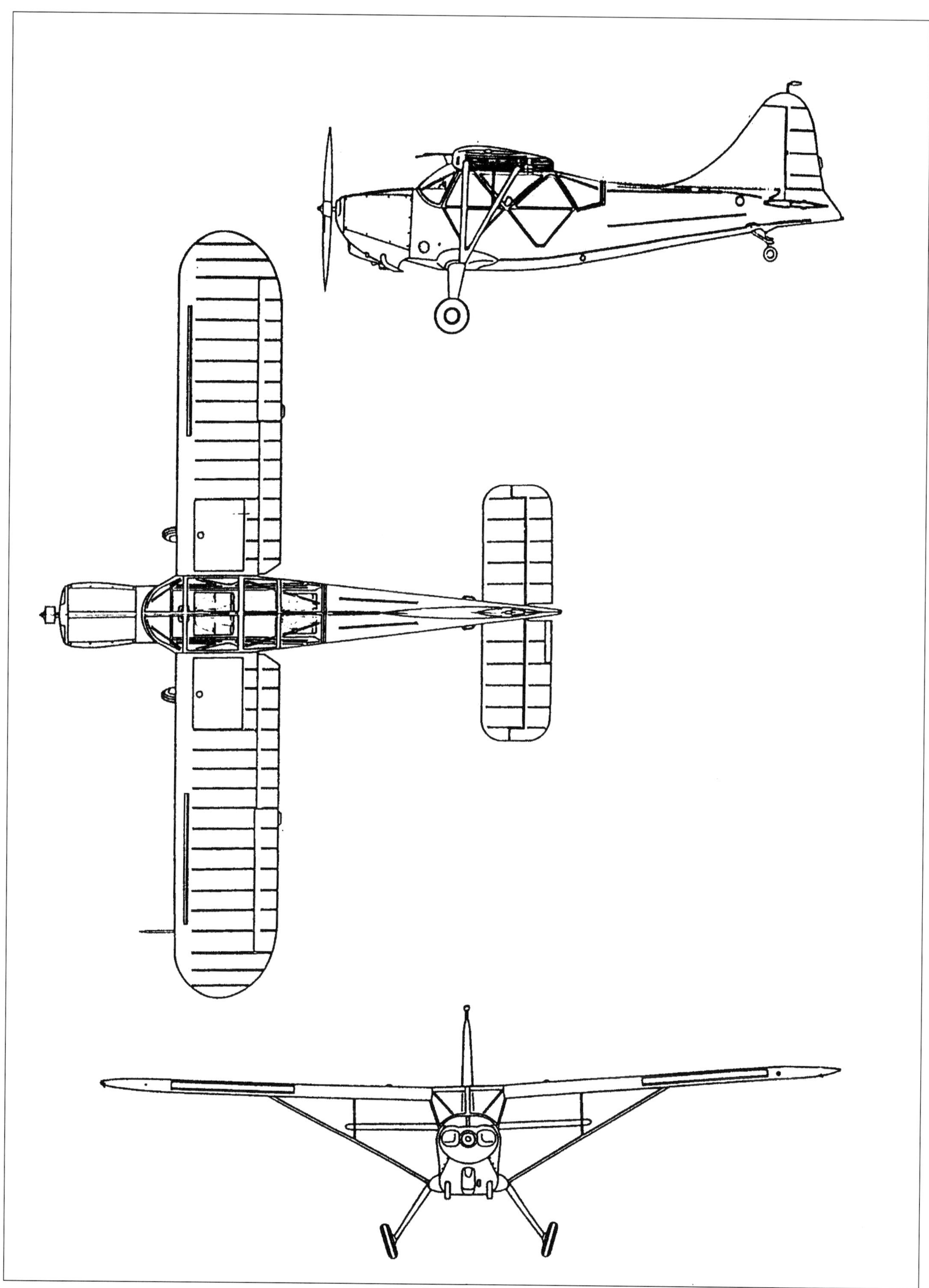

O-54 / L-5

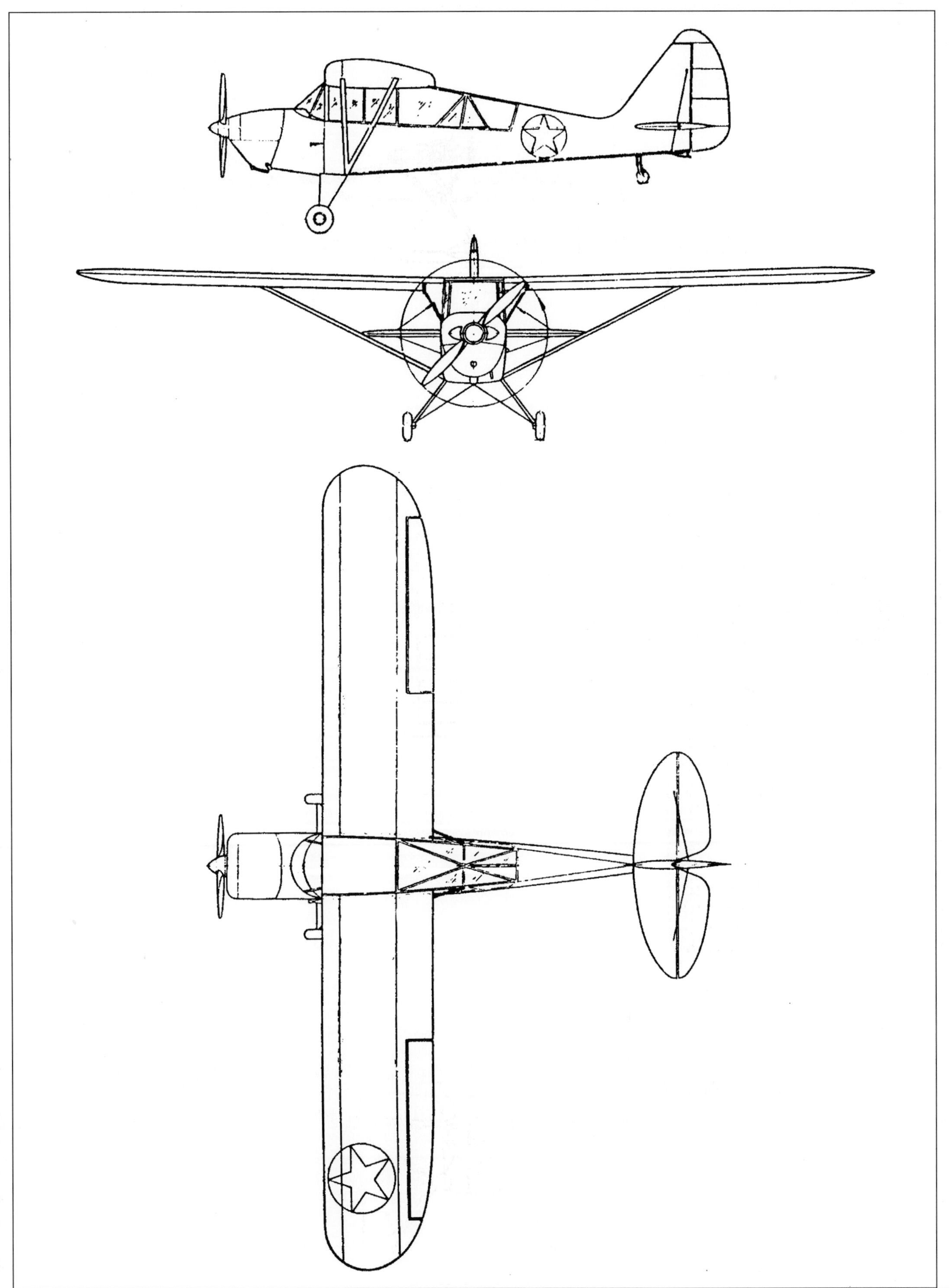

O-63 / L-6

POSTLUDE

The next time you see an old, tired liaison airplane in the back of a hanger or tied down "out of the way," consider and remember and look the old bird over...Glance into the cramped cockpit through the cracked and discolored plastic windows, imagine the excitement and terror of war the little craft once experienced...Visualize a sweaty right hand grasping the "stick," while the left hand is "bending the throttle to the stops," trying to get every ounce of power out of the screaming, red-lined engine as the little plane skims, zig zags, over the tree tops, trying to evade the ever present enemy fighters...Yes, here is a true "warbird"...Legitimate in every sense, as a combat veteran...By modern standards, the old L-Bird may appear frail and may not look like much, but remember this well...In its day, the L-Bird accomplished all that was asked of it and often much more...

Pause and toss a salute to this time-worn war relic and thank God for the men and women who build them, for the men who flew them and maintained the old L-Bird...She has more than your respect...

TERRY M. LOVE

This is the ninth book that Terry Love has written. All had to do with history and most about aviation history. Terry also writes articles for aviation magazines. Terry's deep love for aviation dates back to his first air ride in a Republic Sea Bee at the age of 3-1/2 years. He received his Private pilot's license in 1964 and flew two tours with the U.S. Army in Vietnam aboard Bell UH-ls, deHavilland U-1A Otters, and deHavilland U-6A Beavers. His last tour was in Sikorsky CH-34s helicopters in Germany.

Terry has an Engineering degree from Kansas City College, a B.S. degree in Aeronautics from Parks College of St. Louis University, and a Master's degree in Business Administration from the University of Detroit. He is on his way to earning a Ph.D.

Terry is a member of numerous aviation organizations including 23 years with the Twin City Aero Historians. He is also a member of the international aviation fraternity - Alpha Eta Rho. He presently works for Northwest Airlines in the Minneapolis area. His photo collection is represented in a variety of aviation books and magazines.